READER'S DIGEST

Fast & Fabulous

Low-Sew
Bedroom Projects

READER'S DIGEST

Fast & Fabulous

Low-Sew
Bedroom Projects

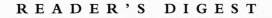

By the editors of *Handcraft Illustrated* magazine

Reader's
Digest

The Reader's Digest Association, Inc.
Pleasantville, New York/Montreal

A Reader's Digest Book

Conceived and edited by the editors of Handcraft Illustrated
Designed by Amy Klee

The acknowledgements and credits that appear on page 126 are hereby made a
part of this copyright page.

Library of Congress Cataloging in Publication Data
Low-sew bedroom projects/by the editors of Handcraft illustrated.
        p.   cm. — (Fast and fabulous)
    Includes index.
    ISBN 0-7621-0028-1
    1. House furnishings. 2. Sewing. 3. Bedrooms 4. Interior
decoration accessories. I. Handcraft illustrated. II. Series.
    TT387.L69   1998   97-31658
    746.9'7—dc21

Reader's Digest and the Pegasus logo are registered trademarks of The Reader's
Digest Association, Inc.

Introduction

There is a sense of settling in when you are in your own bedroom, and there is something restful about being in a bedroom that has been enhanced with personal, handmade touches—ribbon accents that match a color scheme, a lace edge that makes a plain cotton sheet more romantic, or a simple hoop canopy that invites you to sleep and dream beneath it.

This book contains a unique collection of accessories that can be used to transform any bedroom from the ordinary to the extraordinary. Each project requires a minimum of sewing experience and a few hours of time. All of the design ideas included here have two things in common—they are fast and fabulous.

In Chapter One, I've assembled a collection of bedcovers, from a hearty cotton quilt that takes only a few hours to complete, to a simple envelope-style duvet cover that encloses a comforter. The quilt is a patchwork of sturdy cotton napkins in sunshine yellow and cobalt blue, although the combination of colors and patterns can be changed to suit your tastes and style. For the duvet cover, fine cotton sheets are stitched together and accented with ribbon ties to hold your loftiest comforter. For cool nights there is a lap quilt made from velvet. And for the unexpected overnight guest, you'll find a practical and colorful roll-up bed that comes in its own storage sack, perfect for unrolling on the living room couch before the lights are turned out for the night.

Chapter Two indulges in the luxury of the most popular decorative accessory, the accent pillow. Not a necessity, yet an inviting detail on the "bedscape," each pillow uses a unique, yet easy construction technique that transforms it into art. The European pillow sham is made from a recycled bedspread; the sweater and ribbon pillow maximizes the soft-to-the-cheek texture of knitting wool and the elegance of velvet ribbon.

Chapter Three features small touches that take practically no time, add alluring impact to common bed linen, and which enhance the overall design. A white linen pillowcase accented with cord and buttons evokes the feeling of romance, while a simple switch of hems on two different colored pillowcases transforms a basic design to a beautiful one.

Chapter Four presents such accents as a hoop canopy designed to set the mood of an open-air siesta, and a paneled scarf for your dresser. A simple daybed can be made majestic with the look reminiscent of a four-poster bed; a bare floor or worn carpet can be made more romantic and comfortable underfoot with the addition of a velvet floor cloth.

Whether you have a traditional setting, or one that is a combination of hand-me-downs and new pieces, this collection features ideas that you can adapt to your own space, your own tastes, and your own budget. And unlike store-bought articles, these personalized bed covers, linens, and pillows will be custom-made to complement that setting.

Carol Endler Sterbenz
Editor, Handcraft Illustrated

Contents

Pillows

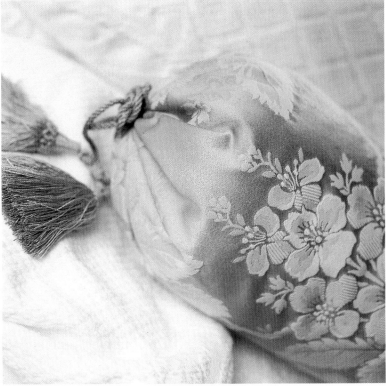

Linens

Bedroom Accents

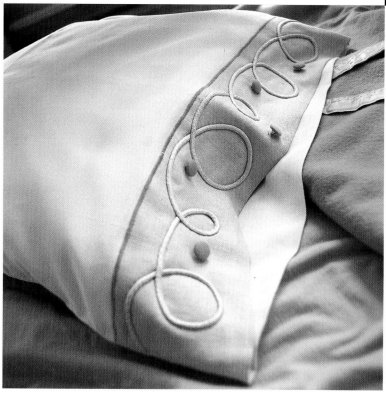

Appendix

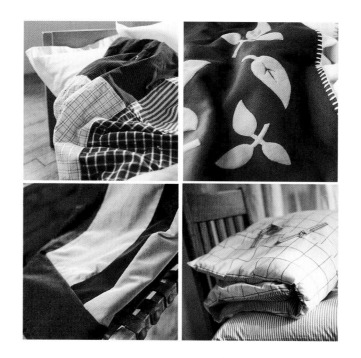

bedcovers

Tufted Napkin Quilt

This lovely patchwork quilt, which brings the warmth of country informality to any room, can be sewn in just a day's time. Instead of using fabric, however, substitute 21in (53.3cm) square dinner napkins to save cutting time. The resulting quilt, with its bright, cheery pattern and simple tufting, adds a cozy appeal when placed at the foot of a bed, or folded and draped across an armchair. To get started, you'll need to purchase 30 napkins. Whatever patterns and colors you choose, the napkins should complement one another. The napkins in this quilt all share a similar style (casual), the same fabric content (100 percent cotton), and coordinating colors. To make the quilt, sew all the napkins together in a pattern, working on one side of the quilt at a time. Then attach the batting to the front of the quilt, and join the two sides together with the batting in between. Finally, tuft the middle of each napkin using embroidery floss in a complementary color.

———

The finished twin-size quilt, assembled from dinner napkins, measures approximately 47 x 78in (1.2 x 2m). For a double-size quilt, add one row of napkins down each side. For a queen-size quilt, add two rows; for a king, add three rows down the sides and one row along the bottom.

MATERIALS

■ **Thirty 21in (53.3cm) square napkins in mixed patterns**

■ **72 x 90in (1.9 x 2.3m) (twin-size) batting**

■ **1 skein embroidery floss**

YOU'LL ALSO NEED:

Matching thread; embroidery needle; sewing machine; scissors or rotary cutter and cutting mat; straight pins; pencil; scrap paper; iron and ironing board; safety pins; laundry detergent; and access to washer and dryer.

SEWING TIP

Slipstitching is used to hand-sew a seam or opening invisibly. To make the stitch take small, even stitches, first from one side of the opening, then the other, through the hem fold. Pull the thread together as you go so that both sides are brought close and form an even seam.

Instructions

1. Prepare napkins. Wash all napkins in cold water, machine-dry, and press well. Using smallest napkin as template, trim all napkins to perfect square.

2. Determine quilt pattern. Position 15 napkins face up on large, flat work surface to form grid measuring 3 napkins across by 5 napkins down. Rearrange napkins as desired, then sketch design on scrap paper. Place napkins in 3 stacks according to 5-napkin columns in grid. Repeat process to create pattern for back of quilt.

3. Sew 5-napkin columns. Place 2 napkins from first stack together, right sides facing, all edges even. Pin along one edge, then stitch ½in (1.3cm) from edge. Repeat to join 3 additional napkins to create one column of 5 napkins (see illustration A, facing page). Repeat process to create 5 additional columns for quilt front and back, referring to sketch as necessary to confirm order. Press all seams open.

4. Sew columns together. Referring to sketch, place first 2 columns for quilt front right sides together. Pin one long edge, then stitch ½in (1.3cm) from edge. Repeat to join third column for quilt front (illustration B). Press seams open. Repeat process for quilt back.

5. Assemble quilt. Position batting on large, flat work surface and place quilt front on top, right side up. To pin-baste quilt, insert safety pin through both layers at center of each square. To mark section for turning, machine baste through both layers ½in (1.3cm) from one short edge for 20in (50.8cm); basting should be placed roughly in the middle of the edge (illustration C). Place quilt back face down on quilt front, edges matching, and secure with straight pins. Machine-stitch ½in (1.3cm) from napkin edges, all around quilt, but leave machine-basted section open for turning quilt right side out. Trim excess batting as close to stitching as possible (illustration D), then clip corners of quilt and batting diagonally. Turn quilt right side out through machine-basted opening, then slipstitch opening closed.

6. Add tufting. Position quilt face up. Thread embroidery

Making the Quilt

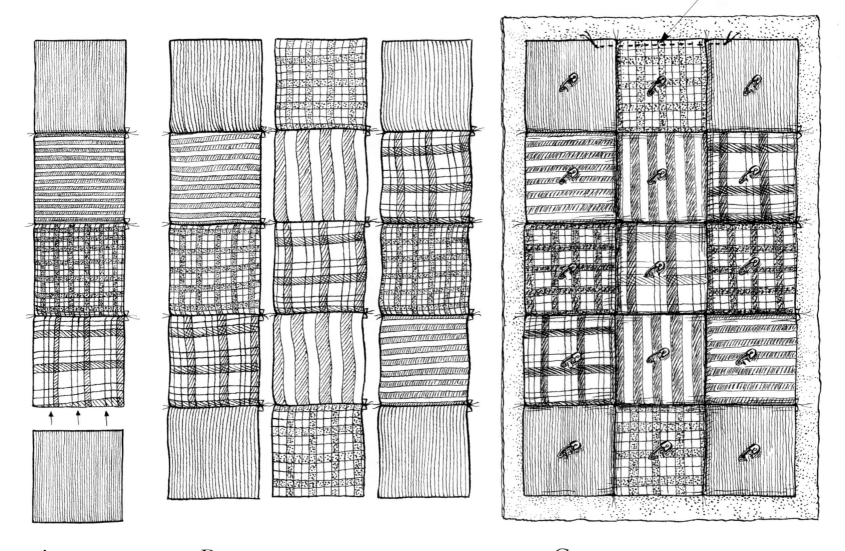

machine baste for 20" (50.8cm)

A. **Sew five napkins together to make a column.**

B. **Sew three columns together to make the quilt front, then sew the remaining three columns together for the quilt back.**

C. **Baste the quilt front to the batting using safety pins, then machine-baste the top edge for 20in (50.8cm).**

15

*To further coordinate your
bedroom furnishings, consider
stitching pillows or other items
from the same pattern.*

needle with 36in (91.5cm) of embroidery floss. Working one
block at a time, remove safety pin, then insert needle down
through center of block and draw out ¼in (.7cm) away. Pull
through, leaving 3in (7.6cm) tail (illustration E). Make second
stitch along same path (illustration F), then draw floss snug and
cut, leaving 3in (7.6cm) end. Tie ends in square knot (illustration
G). Repeat for remaining 14 blocks. Snip excess floss ½in
(1.3cm) from knot to finish quilt (illustration H).

DESIGNER'S TIP

**For variation on this design, make a quilt using two differ-
ent napkins arranged in a checkerboard pattern. For a
fancier version of this quilt, insert edging between the
front and back, such as piping, eyelet, or tassel fringe.**

leave unstitched for turning

*wrong side
(of quilt back)*

D. **Stitch the quilt back face down to the
quilt front, trim away the excess batting,
and turn the quilt right side out.**

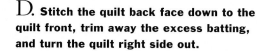

Adding the Tufting

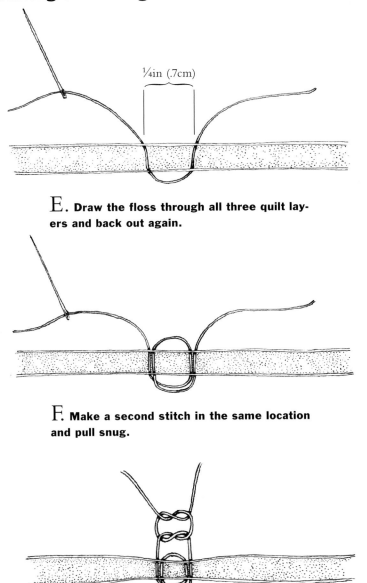

¼in (.7cm)

E. **Draw the floss through all three quilt layers and back out again.**

F. **Make a second stitch in the same location and pull snug.**

G. **Tie the ends together in a tight square knot.**

H. **To finish, trim the excess floss ½in (1.3cm) from the knot.**

Duvet Cover with Tie Closures

All you need to make this beautiful full size duvet cover is a set of coordinated flat sheets. The duvet cover is made like a huge, flapped envelope, held closed by tab ties. The front of the duvet is made from one sheet. The back of the duvet is made from two pieces of the same sheet, which are overlapped in order to create an opening, but then held closed with ties. The sheets we selected feature crisply tailored blue and white shirting patterns, but you can substitute a variety of colors or patterns. One advantage to the stripe and check, however, is that the pieces can be cut along the lines as if they were laid out on a grid. This grid will also help you place the ties evenly. If you choose a large pattern, be sure to center the design on the center of the duvet cover.

——

For a duvet cover such as this one, which measures 66 x 84in (1.7 x 2.1m) you will need one full-size and one queen-size sheet, both with 4in (10cm) top hems. The full-size sheet makes the duvet cover's back; the queen-size sheet makes the duvet cover's front.

MATERIALS

- **1 queen-size sheet**
- **1 color-coordinated full-size sheet**

YOU'LL ALSO NEED:

Duvet; thread; sewing machine; scissors; rotary cutter and cutting mat; straight pins; fabric pencil; marking chalk; yard-stick or right-angled ruler; safety pin; iron; and ironing board.

Instructions

1. Cut duvet cover front and ties. Press queen-size sheet and position on large, flat surface. For front of duvet cover, measure from bottom right corner along small hem 67in (1.7m) and mark with fabric pencil. Measure from same corner along side edge 85in (2.2m) and mark. Complete rectangle with fabric pencil based on these measurements, using right-angled ruler or yardstick. From remainder of sheet, mark strips for tab ties 70in (177.8cm) long by 2in (5cm) wide. Cut all pieces using rotary cutter. Label all pieces on wrong side with chalk.

2. Cut duvet cover back. Press full-size sheet and position on large, flat surface, right side up. To mark for back of duvet cover, measure 67in (1.7m) from bottom left corner along small hem of sheet. Measure 81in (2.1m) from same corner along side edge.

Complete rectangle based on these measurements, using right-angled ruler. Keep small bottom hem intact as part of rectangle. For duvet flap, use 4in (10cm) sheet hem as hem, then measure rectangle 8in (20cm) from edge of hem by 67in (1.7m). Label each piece on full-size sheet, then cut all pieces as marked.

3. Make tab ties. Fold 2in (5cm) strips in half lengthwise, right sides together, edges matching. Stitch ½in (1.3cm) from raw edges along each strip. Roll seam to center top and lightly press seam open. Stitch across each strip every 7in (17.8cm). Using illustration A, page 21, as reference, cut across each strip just to right of stitching to make 20 individual ties. Using eraser end of pencil, turn ties right side out. Press, tucking in raw edges ⅜in (9.5mm) to inside.

4. Mark for ties. Place duvet flap right side up on flat surface. To mark flap for attaching 10 ties, insert pin at center of hemmed edge. Measure 3in (7.6cm) to each side from center pin and insert pins as markers. Remove center pin. Continue marking pins every 6in (15cm) to ends of flap (illustration B). If using stripe, check, or any geometric pattern, adjust measurements between pins as necessary to ensure that pin markers relate to pattern.

5. Attach ties to flap. At each pin, place tie with tucked end overlapping edge of flap ¾in (1.9cm) as in illustration C. To secure tie to flap, topstitch from right side as shown in illustration D. Repeat with remaining ties.

6. Attach ties to back. Position flap and back, right sides up, with hemmed edges of both pieces overlapping by 4in (10cm). Pin flap to back at edges to secure; overall length should match duvet cover front. Fold ties on flap up and off back (illustration E). Position new tie on back, aligned with matching tie on flap. End of tie should fall 1½in (4cm) below edge of flap. Pin tie to back, then pin remaining ties in place. Topstitch ties to back as done on flap piece.

7. Assemble duvet cover. Position back and flap on top of cover front, right sides together and edges matching. Stitch all around using ½in (1.3cm) seams. Turn cover right side out through flap opening. Press. Insert duvet and use ties to close.

Making the Duvet Cover

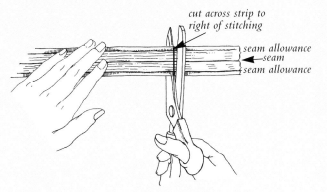

cut across strip to right of stitching

seam allowance
seam
seam allowance

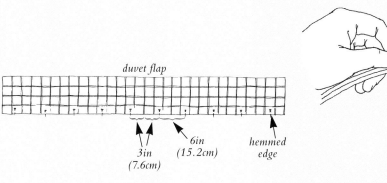

duvet flap

6in
(15.2cm)

3in
(7.6cm)

hemmed edge

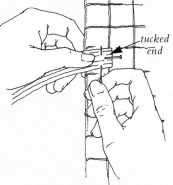

tucked end

A. **Stitch across the strips every 7in (17.8cm), then cut across the strip to make the individual ties.**

B. **Mark the tie position on the flap...**

C. **...then pin the ties in place.**

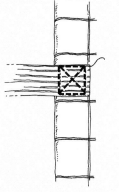

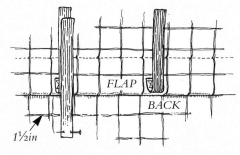

FLAP

BACK

1½in

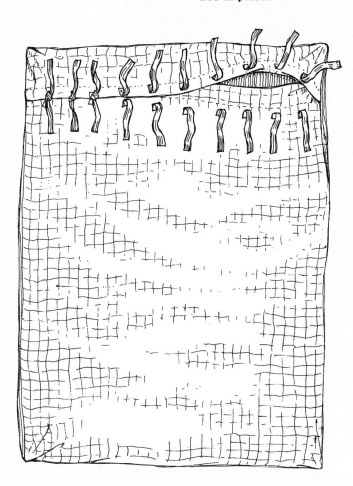

D. **To attach the ties, topstitch the ends as shown.**

E. **Pin flap and back together, then fold ties on flap up and off back (tab on right). Stitch a corresponding tie on back.**

F. **Sew lining and cover together, then turn cover right side out. Insert duvet into cover and tie tabs closed.**

21

Appliqué Blanket Turnover

Looking for a beautiful and unique addition to your guest bedroom? Consider adding an appliquéd turnover to a solid-colored blanket for a subtle yet elegant touch. The appliqué portion of the blanket shows when the top of the blanket is turned down, hence the name "turnover." To get started, you will need an ordinary acrylic or wool blanket. First, cut six leaves from coordinating wool and appliqué them to the section of wool chosen for the turnover. This piece is then folded in half and sewn to the top of the blanket, extending its length by 30in (76.2cm). When the blanket is placed on the bed, the top section is turned back to reveal the appliquéd design.

———

A queen-size wool or acrylic blanket is used for the body of the turnover, and a 30in (76cm)-wide woven wool cuff is added to the top end of the blanket. The appliqués require ⅜yd (32cm) of 60in-(1.5m)-wide woven wool fabric. Fabric requirements and measurements are given for a full/queen-size blanket. Before starting, decide which corner you would like to embellish.

MATERIALS

- **Full/queen-size 90 x 90in (2.3 x 2.3m) woven wool or acrylic blanket**
- **2⅝yd (2.4m) 60in-(1.5m)-wide wool (for turnover)**
- **⅜yd (32cm) 60in-(1.5m)-wide wool (for appliqués)**
- **One skein 4oz (113.6gm) worsted wool yarn (to contrast with blanket)**
- **One skein 4oz (113.6gm) worsted wool yarn (to match appliqué fabric)**
- **Patterns (see page 122)**

YOU'LL ALSO NEED:

Matching cotton thread; clear nylon size .004 monofilament thread; sewing machine with zigzag attachment; cutting shears or rotary cutter and mat; scissors; tape measure; yardstick or see-through grid ruler; tapestry needle; pins; light and dark fabric marking pencils; fabric glue stick; and access to photocopier.

DESIGNER'S TIP

For a different look, slip a contrasting piece of fabric under the vein cutout before you appliqué.

Instructions

1. Cut wool for turnover. Measure width of blanket. Trim selvages from wool selected for turnover and cut to width of blanket (see illustration A, facing page). Cut binding from one end of blanket.

2. Cut out leaves. Photocopy six leaf patterns (page 122), enlarging 200 percent. Cut out patterns, then cut vein outlines. Pin patterns to wool selected for appliqués and cut out, including veins.

3. Appliqué leaves to turnover. Position wool wrong side up on flat surface. Fold top long edge down to meet bottom long edge (illustration B). Rub glue stick onto back of each wool leaf, then arrange leaves on right side of fabric near fold at left corner as shown, and hand-press in place. Unfold turnover carefully. Thread machine needle with clear monofilament thread and bobbin with cotton thread to match turnover. Machine baste leaves to turnover fabric, stitching close to appliqué edge. Set sewing machine for ⅛in (3.2mm)-wide zigzag stitch. Test tension on scrap before stitching turnover; for smoother stitching, loosen upper thread. Appliqué leaves to turnover by zigzagging over all raw edges and covering basting stitches.

4. Join turnover to blanket. Position turnover on flat surface, right side up, with leaves at lower left. Place blanket wrong side up, with turnover overlapping its raw edge by 2in (5cm). Pin in place, then topstitch turnover edge to blanket (illustration C). Turn blanket over. Fold down turnover so edge conceals machine stitching. Zigzag turnover edge to blanket, stitching through all three layers (illustration D).

5. Blanket-stitch edges. Lay grid ruler or yardstick ⅝in (1.5cm) in from side edges of blanket. Using contrasting fabric marking pencil, mark dot along ruler edge every ½in (1.3cm). Thread tapestry needle with 36in (91cm) of yarn to match appliqué fabric. Following dots, blanket-stitch along both edges, inserting needle close to fabric edge, drawing out over standing thread, and pulling snug (illustration E). Join in new yarn when needed, and switch to contrasting blanket-colored yarn when stitching turnover section (illustration F).

Sewing the Blanket

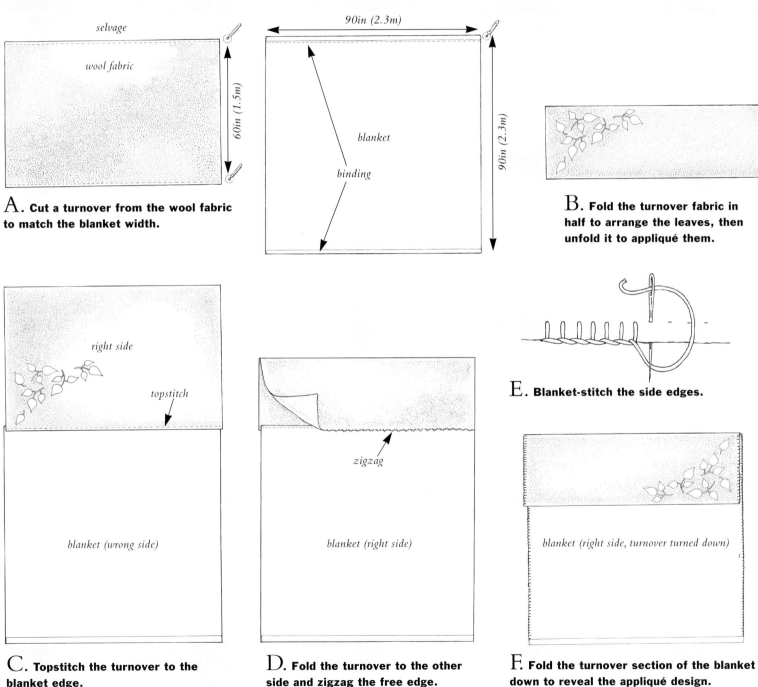

A. Cut a turnover from the wool fabric to match the blanket width.

selvage

wool fabric

60in (1.5m)

90in (2.3m)

blanket binding

90in (2.3m)

B. Fold the turnover fabric in half to arrange the leaves, then unfold it to appliqué them.

C. Topstitch the turnover to the blanket edge.

right side

topstitch

blanket (wrong side)

D. Fold the turnover to the other side and zigzag the free edge.

zigzag

blanket (right side)

E. Blanket-stitch the side edges.

F. Fold the turnover section of the blanket down to reveal the appliqué design.

blanket (right side, turnover turned down)

Velvet Lap Throw

This luxurious tasseled lap throw adds glamour to any bedroom. Drape it casually on a comfortable chair, arrange it on a chaise lounge, or fold it for warmth at the foot of a bed. To get started on this project, select three compatible colors of home furnishing-weight cotton velvet. Two of the colors will be cut and sewn into stripes, then used for the body of the throw, while the third color is used to form a mitered border. When selecting colors, pick one medium shade for the border (we used a rich red), one lighter shade for one stripe (we chose honey), and a darker shade for the second (we liked black). The throw is backed with velvet; we used the same shade on the back as the border. To finish, embellish the corners with buttons and tassels.

———

Because the back is cut in one piece, the size of the throw is determined by the width of the velvet you select. After cutting ½in (1.3cm) selvages away, our velvet had a width of 55in (1.4m); our finished lap throw measures 54in (1.4m) square. If your velvet is narrower, your lap throw and proportion of stripes will be that much smaller, unless you line the back with a wider fabric, such as a challis or cotton damask.

MATERIALS

- 3½yd (3.2m) 55 to 56in (1.4 to 1.5m)-wide red velvet (border and backing)
- 1¼yd (1.4m) 55 to 56in (1.4 to 1.5m)-wide honey velvet (stripe)
- 1¼yd (1.4m) 55 to 56in (1.4 to 1.5m)-wide black velvet (stripe)
- Eight ¾in (1.9cm) button-covering kits
- Four 5in (12.7cm) tassels

YOU'LL ALSO NEED:

Sewing machine; matching thread; cutting shears or rotary cutter and mat; right-angled ruler or yardstick; scissors, hand-sewing needle; light and dark marking pencils; iron; ironing board; velvet pressing board, terry toweling, or extra piece of velvet.

Instructions

1. Cut narrow stripes. Position black velvet on large, flat surface with pile going downward. Cut off one selvage. Measure and cut three pieces 43 x 4in (1.1m x 10.2cm). Notch at center bottom of each strip to indicate that pile is running down towards notch (see illustration A, right).

2. Cut wide stripes. Position honey velvet on large, flat sur-

Cutting the Velvet

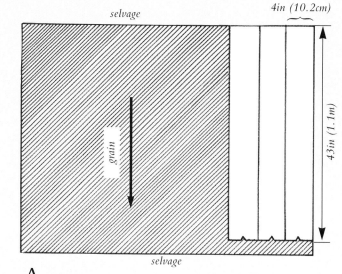

A. **Measure and cut the narrow stripes from black velvet.**

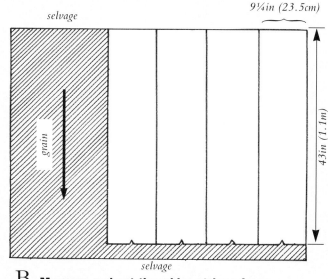

B. **Measure and cut the wider stripes from honey-colored velvet.**

Assembling the Throw

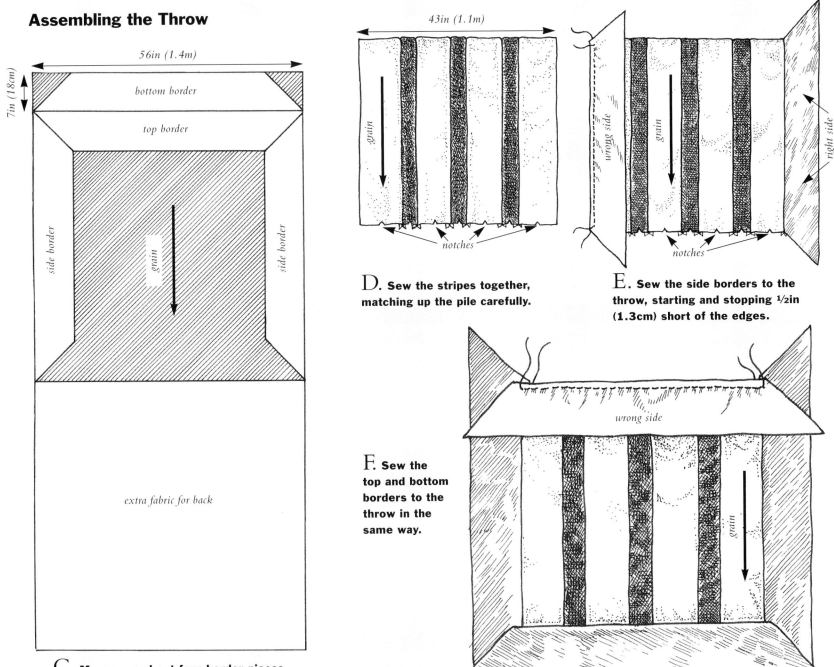

56in (1.4m)

7in (18cm)

bottom border

top border

side border

side border

grain

extra fabric for back

C. **Measure and cut four border pieces from red velvet.**

43in (1.1m)

grain

notches

D. **Sew the stripes together, matching up the pile carefully.**

wrong side

grain

right side

notches

E. **Sew the side borders to the throw, starting and stopping ½in (1.3cm) short of the edges.**

wrong side

grain

F. **Sew the top and bottom borders to the throw in the same way.**

face with pile going downward. Cut off one selvage. Measure and cut four pieces 43 x 9¼in (1.1m x 23.5cm). Notch at center bottom of each strip to indicate that pile is running down towards notch (illustration B). Save leftover fabric for buttons.

3. Cut border. Position red velvet on large, flat surface with pile going downward. Measure and cut two pieces 56 x 7in (1.4m x 18cm). Rotate velvet, then cut two additional pieces the same size with pile going horizontally. Cut ends at 45-degree angle (illustration C). Notch to indicate direction of pile.

4. Sew stripes. Line up all pieces with pile going in same direction. Pin, then stitch wide and narrow stripes together to form 43in (1.1m) square, using ½in (1.3cm) seams (illustration D). Place velvet nap (right side) down on velvet pressing board or on top of napped fabric (terry or velvet). Press seam open.

5. Add border. With right sides facing, pin side borders to sides of square; line up pieces with pile going in same direction. Stitch, starting and stopping ½in (1.3cm) from corners (illustration E). Repeat process for top and bottom borders (illustration F). With right sides facing, pin, then sew adjacent corner flaps together to form diagonal using ½in (1.3cm) seams (illustration G). Press seams open, and trim points at corners of seams (illustration H).

6. Cut velvet back and add tassels. Place remaining red velvet on large, flat surface. Measure and mark perfect 55in (1.4m)

square. Position lap throw front on top to check fit; adjust if necessary, then cut. Notch to indicate direction of pile. Position throw front right side up, then stitch loops of tassels to each corner (illustration I) so tassel faces body of throw.

7. Sew front to back. With right sides facing, pin front to back all around; leave 12in (30cm) gap at a center side for turning. Stitch using ½in (1.3cm) seams. Trim corners. Turn right side out and slipstitch opening closed (illustration J).

8. Finish throw. To make buttons, cover eight ¾in (1.9cm) buttons with scraps of black velvet. Position lap throw face up on large, flat surface. Pin around perimeter ¾in (1.9cm) from edge so velvet backing does not show, then topstitch. Sew button at each inner and outer corner of border (illustration K).

Finishing the Velvet Lap Throw

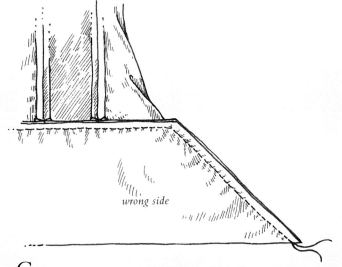

wrong side

G. **Sew the seams at the mitered border corners.**

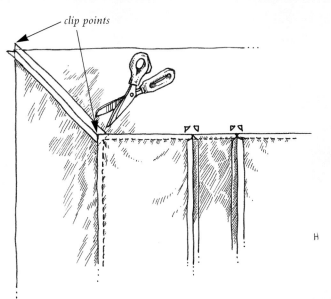

clip points

H

H. **Press open the mitered border seams, and clip the points to prevent bulky seams.**

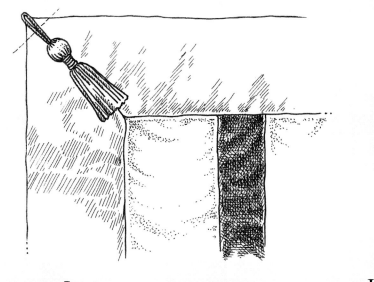

I. **Sew the tassel loops on the corners before attaching the back.**

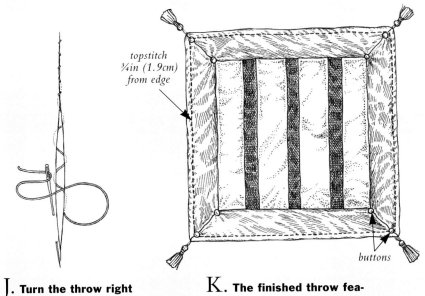

topstitch ¾in (1.9cm) from edge

buttons

J. **Turn the throw right side out and slipstitch the opening closed.**

K. **The finished throw features covered buttons on the corners.**

Roll-Up Bed
with Storage Sack

There are times when a full house means overnight guests must sleep on the sofa. This cozy fleece roll-up bed is designed to roll out on a couch, filling in the gaps between sofa cushions, and making a smooth, comfortable surface to sleep on. To make the bedroll especially thick and inviting, we sewed three layers of batting inside the fleece. When not in use, the bed can be rolled up, secured with a 3in (7.6cm)-wide reversible strap, and slipped inside its satin and fleece storage bag.

———

Polar fleece is a perfect fabric for this project, as it is warm, lightweight, and washable. Many colors and types of fleece are available in fabric stores. We picked three contrasting but compatible colors—sage green and butter yellow for the bed, and coral for the storage bag. To add a touch of decoration, we embroidered simple cross-stitches on the bedroll using yellow yarn.

MATERIALS

Yields two bedrolls 68 x 22in (1.7m x 56cm)

- **2yd (1.8m) sage green fleece**
- **2yd (1.8m) butter yellow fleece**
- **1yd (91.4cm) coral fleece**
- **1yd (91.4cm) 45in-(1.2m)-wide washable gold satin**
- **2yd (1.8m) sage green cotton cord**
- **One package (72 x 90in/1.8 x 2.3m) seamless sheet polyester batting**
- **Small skein 4-ply yellow acrylic yarn**
- **Two size 36 button-covering kits, 7/8in (2.2cm) diameter**
- **Water soluble marking pen**

YOU'LL ALSO NEED:

Sewing machine with zigzag attachment and buttonhole capability; monofilament thread; thread to match fleece(s); cutting shears or rotary cutter and mat; marking pencil; hand-sewing needle; seam ripper; tape measure; ballpoint pen; scissors; thimble; large safety pin; yardstick or right-angled ruler; and large tapestry needle.

Instructions

1. Cut bedroll, straps, and batting. Mark and cut one sage green piece of fleece and one butter yellow piece of fleece measuring 68 x 22in (1.7m x 55.8cm) (see illustration A, page 35). For strap, mark and cut sage green and yellow rectangles of fleece measuring 33¾ x 11in (85.7 x 27.9cm). Fold batting into triple layer and cut rectangle measuring 66¾ x 21¾in (1.7m x 56.4cm).

2. Assemble bedroll. Position sage green fleece on flat surface wrong side up. Center triple layer of batting on top, leaving ⅝in (1.5cm) extra fleece all around edge (illustration B). Turn all over and pin along outer edges. Place butter yellow fleece on flat surface wrong side up. Place sage green piece on top, trapping batting inside and matching raw edges. Pin, then zigzag stitch around all edges using monofilament thread on top and matching thread in bobbin (illustration C).

3. Add cross-stitching and tufting. Use marking pen to mark one line 2in (5cm) in from each short edge, then repeat to create a second line ¾in (1.9cm) further in. Divide into series of ¾in (1.9cm) boxes using additional marks, then cross-stitch using tapestry needle and yarn (illustration D). Place bedroll on flat space and mark eleven places for tufting with pen (illustration E). Using contrasting thread, make 5 stitches in each area, then tie and trim threads.

4. Sew strap. Place both strap pieces together and zigzag around all edges using monofilament thread in machine and bobbin. With leftover scraps, cover two buttons, one in each color. Hand-sew buttons onto strap, one on each side and positioned about ½in (1.3cm) from edge (illustration F). Make buttonhole in center of opposite end of strap.

5. Cut storage bag and lining. On coral fleece, mark and cut circle with diameter of 10in (25.4cm). Fold circle in half, then quarters, and clip on edge at each quarter (illustration G). For body of bag, mark and cut rectangle measuring 33¼ x 28 ½in (84.5 x 72.5cm). At bottom of one long side of bag, clip for ½in (1.3cm) seam allowances. Add clips at center and quarters to

Making the Roll-Up Bed

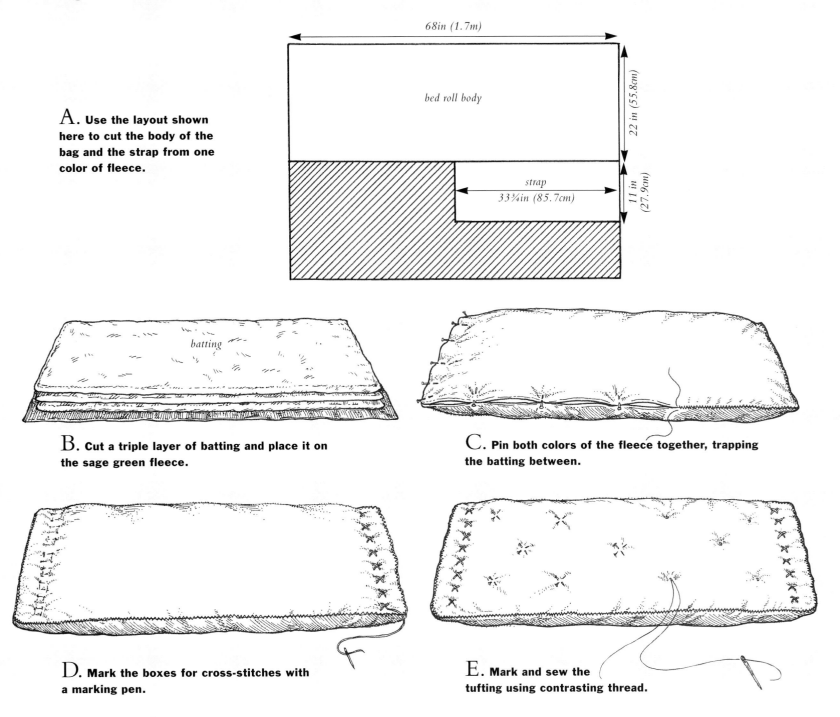

68in (1.7m)

bed roll body

22 in (55.8cm)

strap
33¾in (85.7cm)

11 in (27.9cm)

A. Use the layout shown here to cut the body of the bag and the strap from one color of fleece.

batting

B. Cut a triple layer of batting and place it on the sage green fleece.

C. Pin both colors of the fleece together, trapping the batting between.

D. Mark the boxes for cross-stitches with a marking pen.

E. Mark and sew the tufting using contrasting thread.

Because most polar fleece is made from recycled plastic, it has various properties that affect its use. It should not be ironed, but it can be lightly smoothed—not stretched—into position. In addition, the edges will not unravel, meaning it does not need hemming.

match clips on circle. Cut same size circle and rectangle from lining fabric.

6. Assemble bag. Sew long sides of bag body, right sides together, using ½in (1.3cm) seam. Pin, then stitch circle to bottom edge, right sides facing and notches matching. Turn bag right side out. Repeat process for lining, leaving 6in (15cm) opening in middle of side seam (illustration H) for turning side out. Place fleece bag and lining together, right sides together and raw edges even. Stitch around top raw edge. Trim seam to ¼in (.7cm), then turn bag right side out through lining opening, and slipstitch opening closed (illustration I). Push lining down into bag, then press on lining side around top. To form casing line, stitch 1in (2.5cm) down from top edge. To create opening for cord, undo side seam from topstitching to edge (illustration J). Tie cord to end of safety pin and push closed pin through casing. Knot ends of ties.

7. Roll up bedroll. Roll bed and secure with strap (illustration K). Stuff into bag, pull cord tight, and tie ends.

SEWING TIP

To draw a perfect circle for the end of the bedroll bag, use a 10in (25.4cm) dinner plate or pot cover as a pattern.

Finishing the Roll-Up Bed

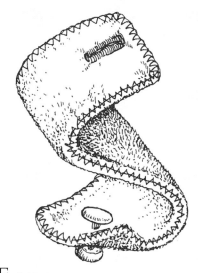

F. **Add the covered buttons at one end of the strap, then make a buttonhole at the opposite end.**

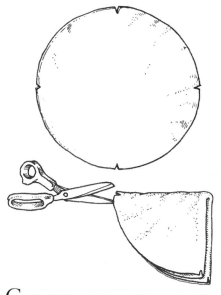

G. **Fold the circle for the end of the bag into quarters, then mark and clip.**

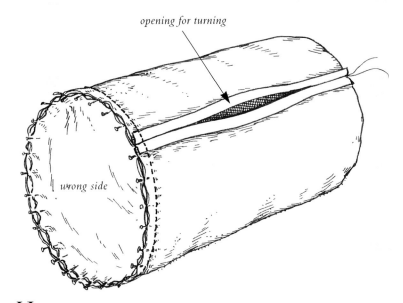

opening for turning

wrong side

H. **Stitch the long edges of the lining rectangle, leaving a gap for turning, then pin and stitch the circle into the lining.**

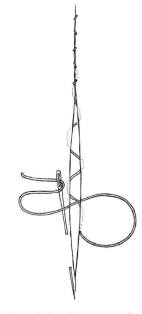

I. **Turn the bag right side out and slipstitch the opening closed.**

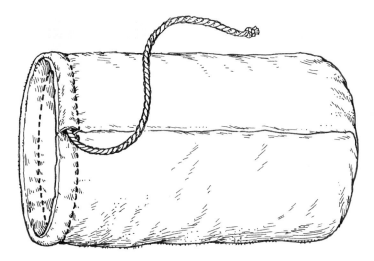

J. **Topstitch a casing for the cord, then undo the seam opening in the casing area to insert the cord.**

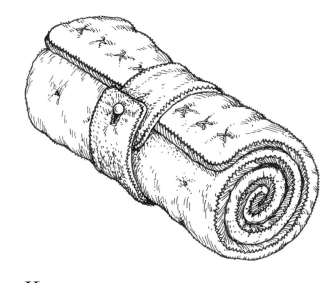

K. **To store the bed, roll it up, button the strap around it, and place it in the bag.**

37

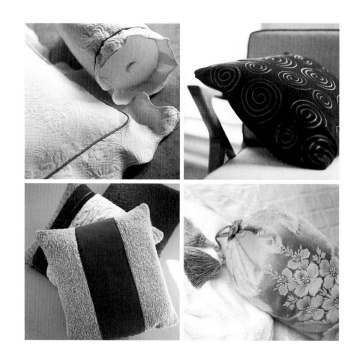

pillows

Slouchy Bedroom Bolster

Soft, touchable fabrics go hand in hand with the casual style of this bolster. Cotton damask has a certain substance, and although it is usually associated with formal rooms, this mint-green damask is used for a slouchy design in an irreverent and pleasing way. Washed in a machine and dried in a dryer, the cotton threads shrink just a bit and create a raised pattern, giving the overall design a shabby chic look. Soft and supple, the damask is slightly oversized to underscore the casual theme.

—

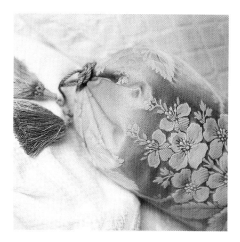

*This bolster cover starts with
a rectangle of fabric that is
sewn to make a tube.
The ends of the tube are
folded over and sewn to create
a casing on both ends
of the pillow; we used a
twisted cord to pull the bolster
cover closed around the
muslin form.*

MATERIALS

- 5 x 15¾in (12.7 x 40cm) muslin bolster form
- ½yd (45.7cm) cotton damask
- 1⅓yd (1.2m) decorative cord

YOU'LL ALSO NEED:

Matching thread; sewing machine; hand-sewing needle;
scissors; yardstick; fabric marking pencil; pins; iron; ironing
board; and grip bodkin or safety pin.

DESIGNER'S TIP

All bolsters have a cylindrical form with a muslin shell
that is filled with feathers (i.e., goose down), synthetic fill
(i.e., polyester fiberfill), or foam rubber. The bolster filling
plays a certain role in determining the character of the
finished pillow: a down-filled bolster is lightweight, soft,
and yielding; a bolster filled with synthetic material is also
soft and lightweight, but typically more dense than one
filled with feathers. A bolster made with a foam rubber
core will retain its shape far better than one with either of
the other fillings, and if wrapped with a layer or two of
fiberfill, batting can also have a softer feeling.

Instructions

1. Cut out rectangle. Place fabric wrong side up on flat surface. Using yardstick and fabric marking pencil and centering any motif, measure and mark 26 x 15¾in (66 x 40cm) rectangle on fabric. Cut on marked lines using scissors. Zigzag all raw edges.

2. Sew bolster cover. Pin and stitch long edges of rectangle, right sides together, then press seam open (see illustration A, facing page). Press raw short edges of tube 1in (2.5cm) to wrong side, then machine-stitch through both layers ¾in (1.9cm) from fold to form casing for cord (illustration B); leave 1–2in (2.5–5cm) opening for inserting casing.

3. Finish bolster. Turn tube right side out and insert bolster form, centering it so excess fabric extends evenly at each end. Using safety pin, thread decorative cord through each casing, entering and exiting at opening. Slipstitch opening closed. Pull cords together and tie securely; let cord ends dangle freely after tying to finish bolster (illustration C).

Making the Bolster Pillow

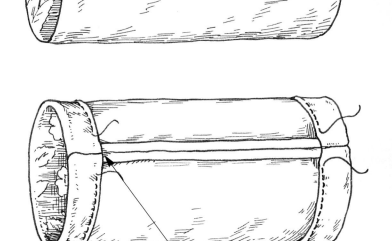

A. Sew the two long edges of the fabric rectangle together.

B. To create a casing at each end, turn the short raw edge to the wrong side, then stitch. Leave a 1–2in (2.5–5cm) opening for inserting the cord.

insert casing here

C. Use a safety pin to insert the cord, then pull the ends together.

European Pillow Sham

Here's a great way to recycle a worn but beloved bedspread: transform it into an oversized pillow sham. The sham shown here was sewn from a matelassé coverlet, incorporating the scalloped edge for a professional-looking silhouette. To add contrast and break up the large field of soft yellow fabric, we introduced a fine, sage green welting between the scalloped border and the sham. To get started, cut the front and the back pieces of the sham. Sew Velcro to the sham's back to form a vertical central closure, then add the welting and flange. Finish the project by stitching the front and back of the sham together.

——

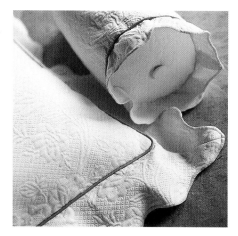

Many bedspread fabrics make wonderful pillows. Consider using candlewick, cotton damask, crisp white cotton seersucker, printed Indian paisley coverlets, lace bedspreads, and vintage quilted spreads.

MATERIALS

- One scalloped matelassé bedspread
- 3yd (2.8m) ready-made welting
- ¾yd (68.6cm) ¾in-(1.9cm)-wide Velcro®
- 26in (66cm) square pillow form

YOU'LL ALSO NEED:

Sewing machine with zigzag attachment and zipper foot; matching thread; yardstick; marking pencil; cutting shears or rotary cutter and mat; scissors; fabric glue; iron; and ironing board.

Instructions

1. Prepare bedspread and cut pillow front. Launder or dry clean bedspread and select best part of bedspread for front of pillow. Mark 28in (71cm) square, centering selected design area and avoiding outer 6in(15.2cm) of bedspread border. Cut out square, then clip at center bottom.

2. Cut pillow back. Cut two 28in (71cm) x 16in (40.6cm) back pieces. On each piece, cut clip at top and bottom 14in (35.6cm) from outer edge to mark Velcro closure at center of sham (see illustration A, facing page). Cut a second clip 1½in (3cm) further along, leaving ½in (1.3cm) to raw edge.

3. Assemble pillow back. Zigzag along one long inner edge to finish inside seam on each piece of pillow back. On flat surface, place one back piece right side up. Position hook portion of Velcro along one edge of back piece (within clips), then stitch along one side of Velcro. Fold Velcro edge to wrong side of pillow back, then stitch along unstitched edge of Velcro (illustration B). Repeat process on second back piece, substituting loop portion of Velcro (illustration C). Press hook and loop sides of pillow back together to form one complete back.

4. Attach welting. Using zipper foot, sew welting to sham front starting at center bottom; leave extra 1in (2.5cm) of welting before notch (illustration D). Clip welting at corners. To finish, leave extra 1in (2.5cm) before trimming welting. Rip welting open approximately 1in (2.5cm) to separate filler cord from fabric. Remove a few stitches and trim cord carefully so ends butt exactly (illustration E). Trim welt fabric to ½in (1.3cm) and fold under raw edge. To finish, stitch welt ends together (illustration F).

5. Cut scalloped border. Measure strips for border 5½in (14cm) wide from outer curve of scallop. Measure 39in (99cm) along outer (curving) edge of scallop (this should equal approximately 26in [66cm] on inner [straight] edge), but add 1in (2.5cm) extra on either side. Cut 2 strips with matched-scallop design from vertical grain, and 2 strips with matched-scallop design from horizontal grain. (The curves at the middle of each border piece should be similar so the scallops will match at the corners.) Mark 45-degree angle at corners.

6. Apply scalloped border. With right sides facing, pin vertical border to sides of pillow front ½in (1.3cm) from corner, taking care to avoid welting. Fold back border corners. Position and stitch horizontal border across top and bottom of pillow using ½in (1.3cm) seams; stop ½in (1.3cm) from corners. Repeat to stitch vertical border (illustration G). Cut away excess fabric at corners (along 45-degree angle), leaving ½in (1.3cm) extra for mitered seams. Position pillow front on flat surface. Pin border miters together on wrong side, starting at exact place where corners converge and making sure border lies flat (illustration H).

Making the Pillow Sham

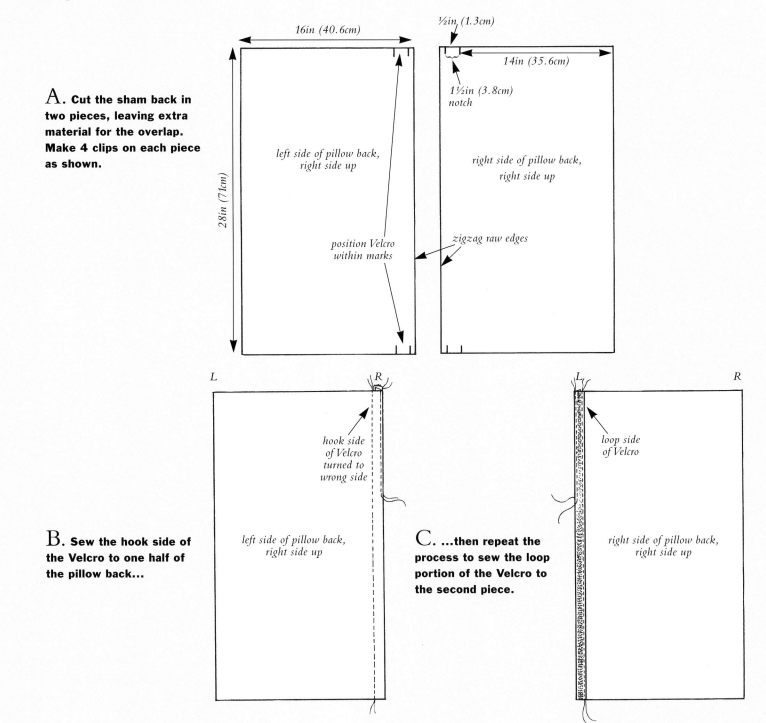

A. Cut the sham back in two pieces, leaving extra material for the overlap. Make 4 clips on each piece as shown.

16in (40.6cm)

½in (1.3cm)

14in (35.6cm)

1½in (3.8cm) notch

28in (71cm)

left side of pillow back, right side up

right side of pillow back, right side up

position Velcro within marks

zigzag raw edges

L   R

hook side of Velcro turned to wrong side

left side of pillow back, right side up

B. Sew the hook side of the Velcro to one half of the pillow back...

L   R

loop side of Velcro

right side of pillow back, right side up

C. ...then repeat the process to sew the loop portion of the Velcro to the second piece.

47

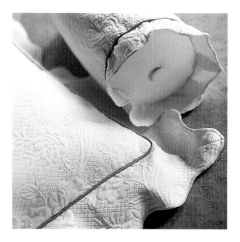

Sew miters, then trim excess fabric. Zigzag raw edges to finish (illustration I). Press mitered seams open.

7. Join pillow front and back. Position pillow front and back together, right sides and bottom notches matching. Fold border inward, between front and back, so raw edges of sham meet, then pin. Stitch around all four edges using zipper foot. Proceed slowly over area where Velcro fastening is located, lifting foot if necessary. Stitch as close as possible to welting, covering previous stitches. Open Velcro and make sure stitching is perfect at mitered corners, then trim. Finish inside raw edges with zigzag stitch, then, if desired, glue down edges using fabric glue.

8. Finish pillow sham. Turn sham right side out. Press corners, if needed. Insert pillow form (illustration J).

Finishing the Pillow Sham

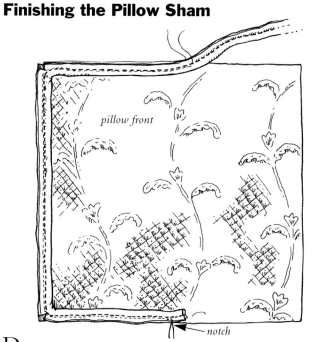

D. **Attach the welting to the sham front, matching the raw edges.**

E. **To join single welt ends, remove a few stitches and cut the cord so ends butt. Trim the welt fabric to ½in (1.3cm) and fold under the raw edge.**

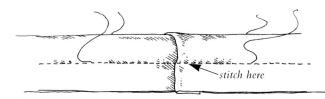

F. **Stitch the ends of the welt together.**

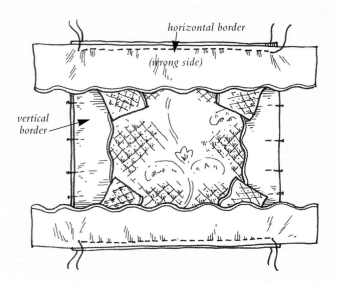

horizontal border

(wrong side)

vertical border

G. **Pin the borders to the pillow front.**

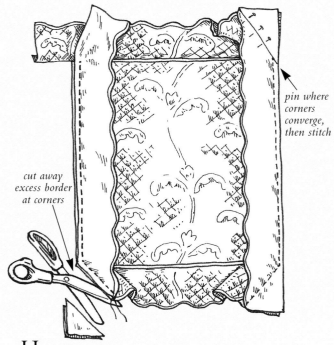

pin where corners converge, then stitch

cut away excess border at corners

H. **Pin and stitch the borders in place.**

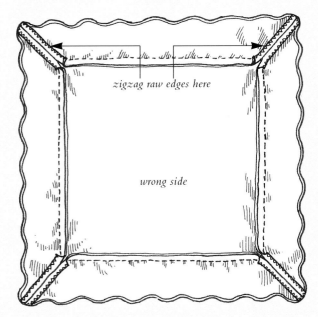

zigzag raw edges here

wrong side

I. **Zigzag the raw edges of the mitered corners to prevent them from unraveling.**

J. **To finish the sham, turn it right side out and insert the pillow form.**

Embossed Velvet Pillow

Velvet's luxury is derived from its nap, the short pieces of fiber that rise above the woven backing of the fabric, alternately absorbing and reflecting light. If you're familiar with velvet, you know that brushing the nap in different directions can create various designs. These pillows beat velvet at its own game. By crushing the nap in very specific places using coils of armature wire (a soft, flexible wire available at craft stores), then setting the impressions with spray starch and an iron, you can create a stunning decorative effect. This technique works with most types of velvet, but this project shines when done on rayon velvet. This technique should not be used on velvet with a stretchy backing, however, as the pattern will get pulled out when the fabric is stretched.

———

Normally, it's undesirable to crush the nap on velvet. This project, however, uses the crushed nap as a decorative accent.

MATERIALS

- ⅝yard (.6m) 45in-(41m)-wide rayon or silk velvet
- 18in (45.7cm) square pillow form
- Thread to match fabric

YOU'LL ALSO NEED:

8ft (2.4m) ⅛in (3.2mm) armature wire; spray starch; 2-qt (1.9liter) plain clean, flat bottom pot; iron; rotary cutter; wire cutters; sewing machine; scissors; hand-sewing needle; ruler; and 8in (20.3cm) square cotton fabric.

> ### DESIGNER'S TIP
> You can use a wide variety of items to "emboss" velvet, including metal house numbers, cut pieces of chipboard, or other heat-resistant materials.

> ### DESIGNER'S TIP
> Some canned spray starch leaves a flaky residue. In our tests, however, we circumvented this problem (and saved money) by mixing our own spray starch. To do this, mix liquid starch and water in a 1:1 ratio, then put the mixture in a spray bottle.

Instructions

1. Make wire spirals. Cut 45in (1.1m), 30in (76.2cm), and 18in (45.7cm) lengths from armature wire. Bend into flat coils measuring approximately 5in (12.7cm), 4in (10.2cm), and 3in 7.6cm) in diameter, respectively (see illustration A, page 53).

2. Emboss velvet. Using rotary cutter, cut two 18in (45.7cm) squares from velvet. Heat iron to hottest (linen) setting. Do not use steam. Set pot face down on ironing board, then set coil on pot bottom (illustration B). Lay velvet over coil, right side down. Apply spray starch liberally (illustration C). Lay cotton fabric on velvet and press with hot iron 10 seconds (illustration D). Carefully lift and reposition iron until entire coil area has been pressed. Repeat process with different-sized coils to create random design over both velvet squares.

3. Assemble pillow. Place velvet squares right sides together, edges matching. Stitch all around, ½in (1.3cm) from raw edges leaving 9in (22.9cm) opening along center of bottom edge for turning. Clip corners with scissors, turn right side out, and insert pillow form. Slipstitch opening closed.

Embossing the Velvet

A. Bend the armature wire into flat coils.

B. Place the coil on an overturned pot.

C. Lay the velvet down on the coil and apply starch.

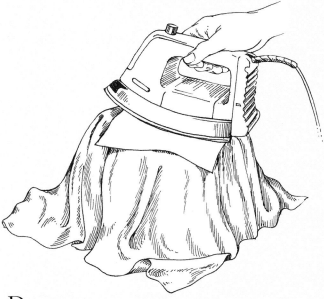

D. Press the velvet with a hot iron to emboss the coil design.

Silk Ribbon Roses

This simple rolling technique transforms wire-edged ribbon into realistic and shapable roses. Use a tiny spray of roses to decorate a blanket as shown, or make large cabbage-style blooms to accent a pillow and small roses for use on a picture frame. To form the rose, roll the interior petals along the ribbon edge, then hand-tack the base of the petals with needle and thread. You can tack the rose to soft furnishings with a needle and thread or use a hot-glue gun for other surfaces, such as frames or boxes.

———

If you combine a series of roses in a cluster configuration, vary the ribbon widths and the bud fullness, and use complementary colors. Solid colors show off the flower form, and ribbons from one color family make the best-looking arrangements.

HOW MUCH RIBBON DO YOU NEED?

Use this chart to determine how much ribbon is needed to make roses and leaves using standard ribbon widths.

Ribbon Width	Ribbon Length Needed	
	Per Rose	Per Leaf
⁷⁄₈in (22.4mm)	10in (25.4cm)	3in (7.6cm)
1¹⁄₂in (3.8cm)	18in (45.7cm)	4in (10.2cm)
2¹⁄₂in ((5.7cm)	24in (61cm)	6in (15.2cm)

MATERIALS
- **One or more rolls wire-edged ribbon**

YOU'LL ALSO NEED:
Wire; scissors; hand-sewing needle; and thread.

OPTIONAL ITEMS:
Hot-glue gun and green florist's tape.

DESIGNER'S TIPS
Make a small bouquet of roses by inserting a wire stem into each rose base, then wrapping it with green florist tape. To make clusters of roses, combine ribbon leaves and inexpensive flocked leaves in several sizes.

Instructions
Making the Rolled Rose
1. Make bud. Unfurl ribbon as needed directly from roll without cutting. Fold end diagonally so tail length equals ribbon width (see illustration A, facing page). Fold tail section in half so right edge of ribbon folds over and meets left edge (illustration B). Fold in half again and using long length of thread, hand-tack at base or gather edges through all layers (illustration C). Do not cut thread at this time.

2. Make petals. Fold excess ribbon back diagonally, then roll tacked portion of rose tightly around corner and onto ribbon edge (illustration D). Once folded edge is wrapped completely around bud, forming small cone, hand-tack base as in Step 1 (illustration E). Repeat folding, rolling, and tacking process to add more petals (illustration F). As rose grows in size, make diagonal folds longer to create larger petals (illustration G).

3. Finish rose. Once rose reaches desired size, cut ribbon, leaving 2in (5cm) tail. Hand-sew running stitch along cut edge, pull to gather, and tack to base of rose (illustration H). Trim excess fabric from base of rose to finish (illustration I).

Making the Folded Leaf
1. Cut and fold ribbon. Cut appropriate length of ribbon (see chart, left) for each leaf. Fold ribbon ends diagonally from top center so tails are equal (illustration J). Fold each tail in half so right edge of ribbon folds over and meets left edge toward center (illustration K), then in half again (illustration L).

2. Finish leaf. Secure folds by binding wire around tails near base of leaf. Twist wire in tight spiral and clip ends to finish leaf (illustration M).

Making the Silk Ribbon Roses

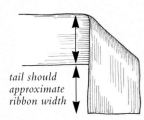

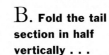

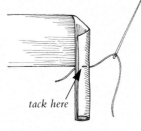

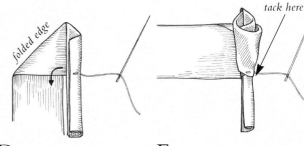

A. Fold down the ribbon end diagonally so the tail extends one ribbon width.

tail should approximate ribbon width

B. Fold the tail section in half vertically . . .

excess ribbon

C. . . . and in half again to make a bud. Tack the bud at the base through all layers.

tack here

D. Fold the excess ribbon back diagonally, then roll the folded bud in the direction of the arrow as shown.

folded edge

E. Stop rolling when the folded edge surrounds the bud. Tack the base again.

tack here

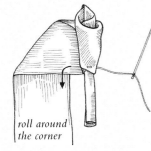

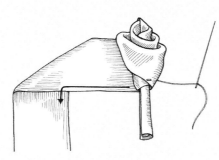

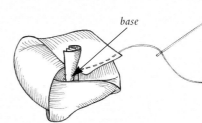

F. Fold the excess ribbon back and repeat the rolling and tacking process to add new petals.

roll around the corner

G. To make the larger, outermost petals, increase the length of the diagonal fold.

H. To finish the rose, cut the ribbon, leaving a 2in (5cm) tail. Turn the rose upside down, hand-sew a running stitch along the cut edge, pull to gather, and tack it to the base of the rose.

base

I. Finished rose.

Making the Leaf

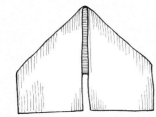

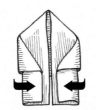

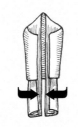

J. Cut a piece of ribbon, then fold down the ends diagonally so the edges are even.

K. Fold each tail section in half toward the center . . .

L. . . . and in half again.

M. Wind thin wire around the leaf base and twist it until secure.

57

Sweater and Ribbon Pillow

When old sweaters become torn or moth-eaten, you can recycle the usable sections by making pillow covers. Sweaters have a warm, textured look that is perfect for a bedroom. Here we mixed cable and bouclé knits, but a simple stockinette stitch would also work well. Vary the colors and knit patterns so they relate to your bedroom decor, and enhance the effect by adding velvet ribbons or bands of velveteen.

—

Making sweater pillows is a simple process, but you will need zigzag capability on your sewing machine. Having selected the sweaters, the size of your pillows will depend on the usable material. Cut a piece of batting to the dimension you've selected and use it as a template. Then sew the sweater pieces together.

MATERIALS

- **Sweaters**
- **Velvet ribbon**
- **Plain cotton velveteen**
- **Batting**
- **Fiberfill or pillow form**

YOU'LL ALSO NEED:

Matching thread; straight pins; sewing machine with zigzag capabilities; cutting shears or scissors; yardstick or right-angled ruler; hand-sewing needle; marking chalk; iron; and ironing board.

DESIGNER'S TIPS

If you have sweater scraps left over, make small pillows and trim with narrow velvet ribbon, or make sachets by filling them with potpourri.

For variation on these designs, use the buttoned-up front of a cardigan sweater, combine fair isle, argyle or other colorful sweaters, or substitute grosgrain ribbon for velvet ribbon.

SEWING TIP

When selecting sweater pieces, consider the sweater's arms, which usually show less wear than the body. Once these are opened up and spread out, they can provide a surprisingly large amount of sweater fabric.

Instructions

1. Prepare sweaters. Cut open at seams and lay pieces flat. Decide on general design by positioning sweaters and velveteen in bands or blocks.

2. Cut batting. On flat surface, cut batting to dimensions of pillow form plus ½in (1.3cm) for seams. Taper corners (see illustration A, facing page). Use batting as template to cut pillow back from velveteen. Position sweater pieces and velveteen on batting. When satisfied with design, mark dimensions of batting on sweater pieces and velveteen with marking chalk and cut (illustration B). Pin pieces temporarily onto batting to double-check accuracy. Turn batting over and trim any protruding edges. Remove pins.

3. Sew pillow. Overlap sweater pieces slightly, then zigzag pieces together. Center and pin ribbon on top of seam and top-stitch in place to cover seams. When design is complete, sew to batting (around edges only) with regular machine stitch (illustration C). With right sides together, pin plain velveteen back to pillow front and sew around all edges using ½in (1.3cm) seams and leaving a 10in (25.4cm) opening at center bottom for turning.

4. Finish pillow. Turn pillow right side out. Insert pillow form or loose fiberfill, then slipstitch opening closed.

Making the Sweater Pillow

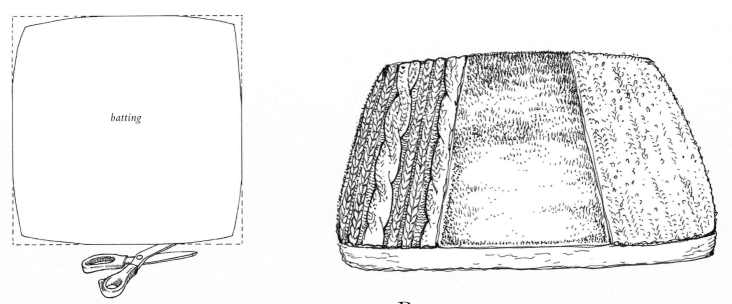

A. When cutting square or rectangular pillows, trim the corners diagonally to prevent pointy corners.

B. Position the sweater pieces and the velveteen on the batting, then mark and cut.

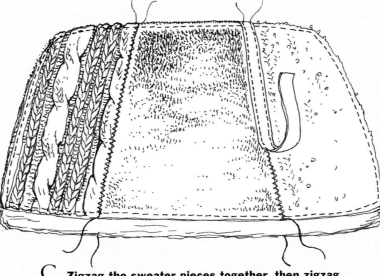

C. Zigzag the sweater pieces together, then zigzag the velvet ribbon on top to cover the seams.

Recycled Bedspread Pillow

Bedspreads are almost always sewn from certain special fabrics, be it tufted candlewick, seersucker, or chenille. And with good reason: These fabrics have a texture and comfort level all their own. You can enjoy that same feeling in another way by using these fabrics to stitch an oversized bedroom pillow such as the one shown here. For variation, select a heavy pique, damask, or white-on-white vintage quilt to complement your bedroom decor.

———

For variation on this design, trim the pillow with moss fringe, a silky, block-cut fringe measuring about 1in (2.5cm) wide. Double it up for a more luxurious effect.

MATERIALS

- One 22in (56cm) square pillow form
- ¾yd (1.4m) 45in (1.1m)-wide bedspread-style fabric
- 2½yd (2.3m) fringe

YOU'LL ALSO NEED:

Matching thread; sewing machine; cutting shears or rotary cutter and mat; scissors; yardstick or right-angled ruler; hand-sewing needle; pins; marking pencil; iron; and ironing board.

Instructions

1. Cut fabric. Position fabric wrong side up. Working along vertical and horizontal grains of fabric, measure and mark 23in (59cm) perfect square. Measure 5¾in (14.6cm) from each corner and mark sides with pencil. Measure in from corner 1in (2.5cm). Join with previous mark to slant off along sides (see illustration A, facing page). Repeat at all corners. Cut front and back of pillow fabric, and mark or notch center bottom of each piece.

2. Apply trim. Position fringe on pillow front, right side down, with woven edges of fringe even with cut edges of pillow fabric. Leaving 1in (2.5cm) extra fringe at notch, start stitching 1in (2.5cm) beyond mark or notch. Stitch fringe all around perimeter of pillow (illustration B), making small notches at corners. Overlap fringe at ends so join looks seamless and stitch over ends of cord (illustration C).

3. Assemble pillow. Position pillow back and front, right sides together, and matching marks or notches. Pin at corners, then pin side seams. Stitch, covering previous line of stitches; leave 15in (38cm) opening at center bottom for turning. Turn pillow right side out, insert pillow form, then slipstitch opening closed using double thread (illustration D.)

DESIGNER'S TIPS

For a vintage look, dye the fabric in tea before stitching. For a softer, more rounded look, make gathered corners, also known as French or Turkish corners. To do this, cut the corners of the pillow cover, and gather or pleat them tightly across the slanted corner before applying the trim. Add a matching tassel at each corner.

Making the Recycled Bedspread Pillow

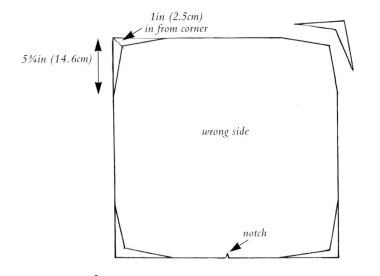

1in (2.5cm) in from corner

5¾in (14.6cm)

wrong side

notch

A. **To prevent flared corners, trim the corners of the pillow cover before stitching.**

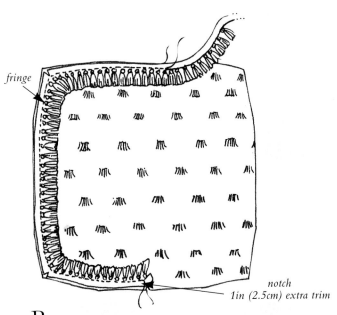

fringe

notch 1in (2.5cm) extra trim

B. **Stitch the fringe to the pillow cover, notching at the corners.**

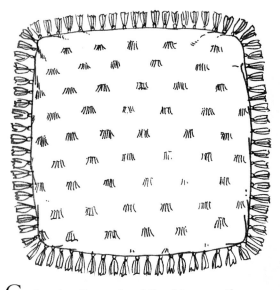

C. **Overlap the ends of the fringe so the seam is almost invisible.**

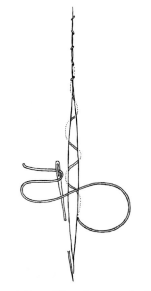

D. **Insert the pillow form and slipstitch the opening closed.**

65

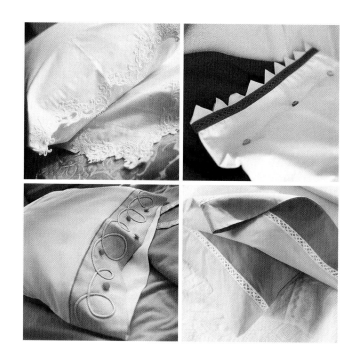

linens

Cutwork Sheet and Pillowcase

Use this exquisite cutwork sheet and pillowcase set to transform an ordinary bedroom into a romantic hideaway. The idea is simple: sew bridal-shop lace motifs onto a plain white sheet and pillowcase, then cut away the underlying fabric to reveal the delicate, scalloped edge.

———

When purchasing your sheet and pillowcase, look for plain, good-quality linens, without fancy hems or piping. A white-on-white look gives the most luxurious effect, but you can apply white lace to colored linens or use colored lace on white sheets as long as both are washable.

MATERIALS

- Plain white pillowcase
- Plain white sheet
- 2 matching pairs of lace motifs

YOU'LL ALSO NEED:

Sewing machine with zigzag capabilities; fine-pointed scissors; matching thread; straight pins; plain white paper; hand-sewing needle; iron; and ironing board.

DESIGNER'S TIP

For variation on this design, set several shapes along the edge of the hem, or combine four or five small, varying motifs, such as hearts and flowers. Make sure all the motifs touch at some point before cutting the edge away.

DESIGNER'S TIP

Lace insertions and appliqués can be found in craft stores, fabric shops, or bridal supply shops. Ours are designed for the neck of a bridal gown, giving them a graceful cut edge. Look for motifs that can be placed in a straight line along the pillow's edge, and at a right angle to each other for the sheet's corner.

Instructions

1. Prepare pillowcase and sheet. Remove labels from pillowcase and sheet, pull out all label threads, and press.

2. Attach lace to pillowcase. Fold pillowcase in half lengthwise and place pin at center edge of one side of open end hem where embroidered motifs will meet. To prevent puckering, position plain white paper under edge of pillowcase hem. Position motifs on either side of center, then pin through hem, lace, and paper. Hand-baste motifs through all three layers in place using large stitches and removing pins as you go (see illustration A, facing page).

3. Sew lace to pillowcase. Thread machine with matching thread. Set machine to ⅛in (3.2mm) wide stitch and close zigzag. Taking care not to catch hem on other side of pillowcase, zigzag over lace motifs, following curves of motif and turning work as you go (illustration B). Remove pillowcase from sewing machine and tear away paper from wrong side.

4. Cut away pillowcase. Turn pillowcase inside out. Using fine-pointed scissors, carefully trim away fabric at edge, working as close to stitches as possible without cutting stitches (illustration C). Cut away any other parts of design, then press.

5. Add lace to sheet. Repeat process for sheet, but place motifs on top corner of sheet at right angle (illustration D).

Making the Sheet and Pillowcase

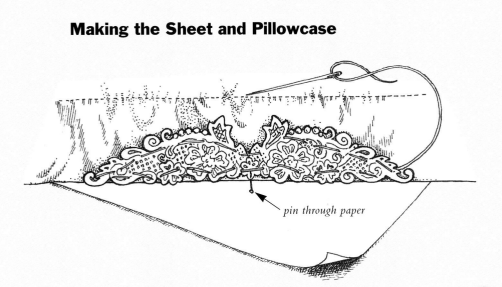

pin through paper

A. **Pin the lace motifs to the fabric through the typing paper, then hand-baste in place.**

B. **Zigzag over the motif, following the curves and turning the work as you go.**

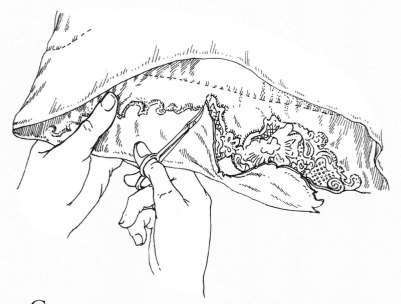

C. **Trim the fabric away from underneath the lace motif.**

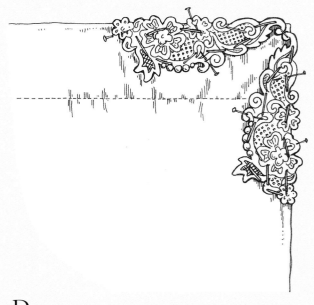

D. **Repeat the process for the sheet, but place the lace motifs on the top corner at a right angle.**

Cord and Button Pillowcase

For a unique pillowcase with a modern look, consider this cord and button pillowcase, sewn in white and tan linen and trimmed in soft, contemporary colors.

We started by cutting the fabric for the decorative pillowcase into two main pieces, and joining them with a seam across one end and down each long side. The contrasting applied hem, with its tubular cord loops, is trapped with a clean finish into the side seams. The cord and buttons are sewn on two thicknesses, that of the contrasting fabric plus the fabric of the pillowcase underneath, which serves as an interfacing to give support. The decorative band heading is self-lined to give a clean finish inside and is held in place with a complementary-colored satin stitch. The back edge of the pillowcase is folded in to form a loose flap hem, into which the pillow form can be tucked so as not to show when in use.

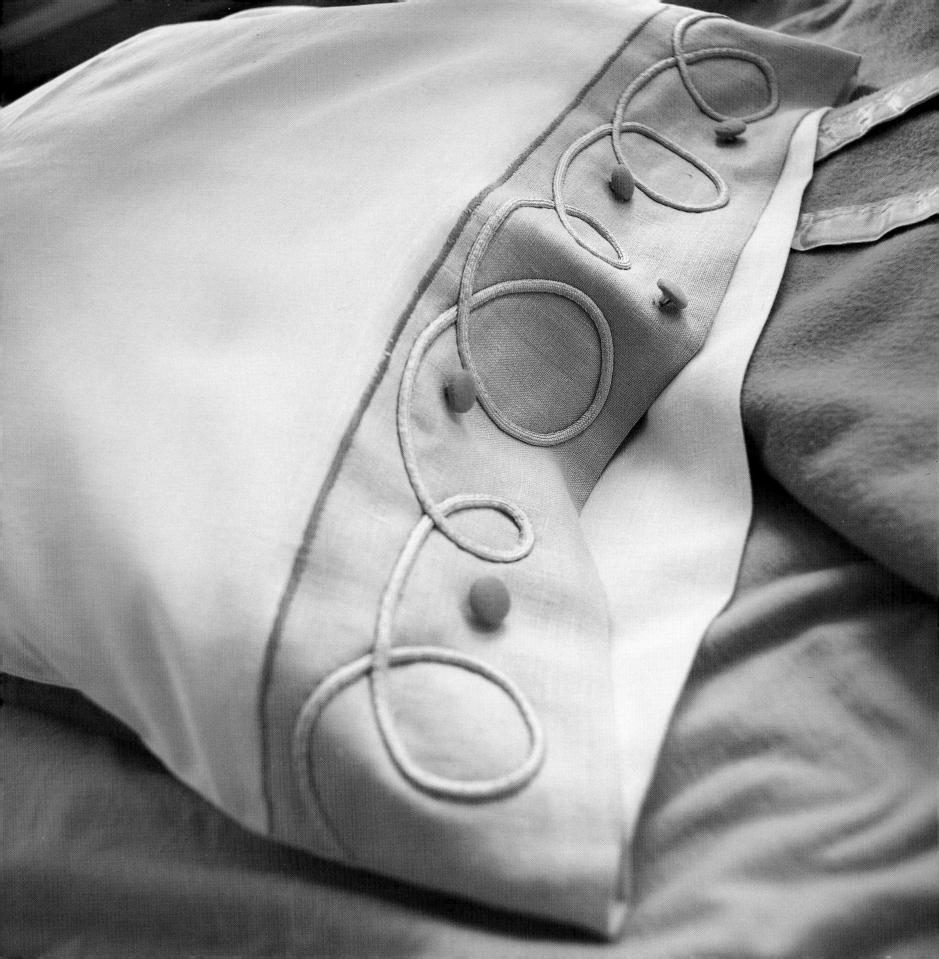

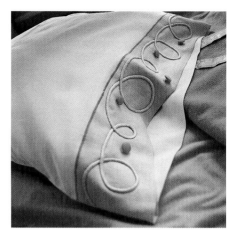

This piece is best dry-cleaned or hand-laundered. For pieces that take less wear, consider sewing a decorative European-size pillowcase, or a smaller boudoir pillowcase. Follow the same directions but adapt the given measurements.

MATERIALS

- **1yd (91.5cm) 45 to 60in-(1.1 to 1.5m)-wide white linen**
- **¼yd (22.9cm) 45in-(1.14m)-wide tan linen**
- **2yd (1.8m) ¼in-(6.4mm)-diameter decorative covered cording**
- **Eight (or more) ⅝in (15.9mm) fabric-covered buttons**

YOU'LL ALSO NEED:

Sewing machine with zigzag attachment; matching thread; complementary thread; monofilament thread; yardstick or right-angled ruler; marking pencil; tracing paper; hand-sewing needle; iron; and ironing board.

Instructions

1. Cut decorative pillowcase body. Establish cross-grain of white linen by pulling thread. For pillowcase front, mark rectangle measuring 21 x 30½in (53.3 x 77.5cm) along vertical grain. For back, mark rectangle measuring 21 x 35½in (53.3 x 90.2cm) along vertical grain (see illustration A, page 75). Cut out both rectangles. Measure down 4in (10.2cm) from top corners of both pieces and mark on the long sides.

2. Cut contrasting front hem. Establish cross-grain of tan linen by pulling thread. Mark and cut rectangle measuring 21 x 8¼in (53.3 x 21cm) along horizontal grain. Fold strip wrong sides together lengthwise, so one long edge measures ¼in (6.4mm) away from other long edge (illustration B). Press.

3. Sew hem to front. Open fold in linen hem. Position linen hem face up on right side of pillowcase front, matching top 4in (10.2cm) of tan linen with marks along side of pillowcase front; bottom edge of pillowcase front should lay in fold of linen. Pin across top edge of linen, then edge-stitch from mark to mark, and down side seams (illustration C).

4. Plan embroidery. Rough out size and number of cord loops using pencil and tracing paper.

5. Zigzag cording. Referring to sketch as needed, pin cording in looped design (illustration D). Thread machine with monofilament thread. Using large, widely spaced zigzag stitch, sew over top of cord following design, stopping ½in (1.3cm) from ends. When design is complete, pull ½in (1.3cm) of filler out of cording fabric at either side, and cut away (illustration E). Straighten out cording.

6. Sew hem to pillowcase. Zigzag across raw edge of linen. Fold hem to wrong side of pillowcase front and pin in place. Sew in place with straight stitch, using first edge-stitch as guide. Thread machine with complementary thread and cover straight stitch with narrow, closely packed zigzag; stitch should appear as one solid satin-stitched line (illustration F).

7. Assemble pillowcase. Press ½in (1.3cm) hem all around pillowcase back, then topstitch with white thread. Position pillowcase front and back together, right sides facing. Using ½in (1.3cm) seams, sew across end without hem. Pin sides. Fold white linen hem over tan linen hem to form flap, and sew sides (illustration G). Finish seams inside with zigzag stitch, trim loose threads, and turn pillowcase right side out.

8. Sew on buttons. Arrange buttons between cord loops on hem, and sew in place (illustration H). Press pillowcase.

Making the Cord and Button Pillowcase

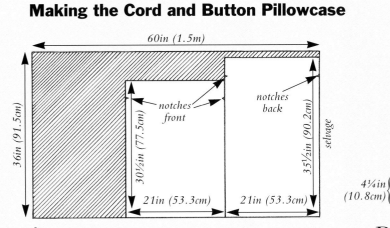

A. Mark and cut white linen rectangles for the pillowcase front and back.

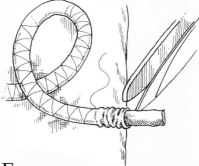

B. Cut the tan linen into a rectangle for the contrasting band, then fold the piece in half.

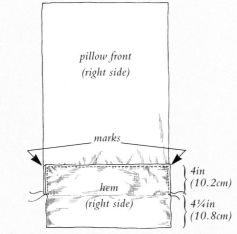

C. Position the opened hem on pillowcase front piece. Pin, then edge-stitch along the sides and across mark to mark (see step 1).

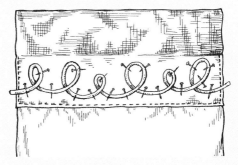

D. Sketch a design on tracing paper, then pin the cord in place on the hem, referring to the sketch as needed.

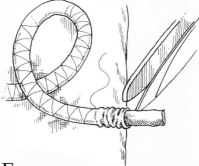

E. Zigzag over the cord using monofilament thread. At the edges, cut ½in (1.3cm) from the filler cord to lessen the bulk at the seams.

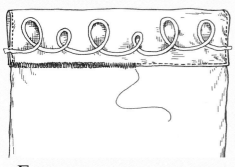

F. Use a line of satin-stitch to hide the seam between the tan linen hem and the main part of the pillowcase.

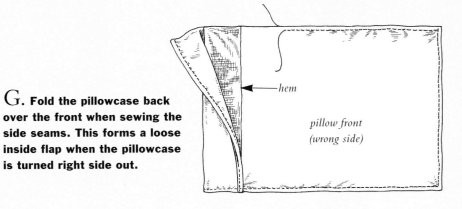

G. Fold the pillowcase back over the front when sewing the side seams. This forms a loose inside flap when the pillowcase is turned right side out.

H. Sew the buttons in place between the cord loops along the hem.

75

Folded Ribbon Pillowcase

Here's a quick way to use folded ribbon to decorate an otherwise plain pillow-case. Start by selecting a good-quality, plain pillowcase with no piping or other trimming. Then choose one or more colors of washable ribbon to complement your bedroom décor. We used several fine grosgrain ribbons, which are partic-ularly easy to fold across the grain. On our pillowcase, the yellow ribbon that forms the points measures 1 1½in (4cm) wide, which allows for exactly nine points on each side of the pillowcase hem. The red ribbon measures ⅞in (2.2cm) wide and covers the stitching that holds the yellow points in place. To soften and enhance the final effect, we stitched a ⅞in-(2.2cm)-wide lavender crochet braid over the red ribbon, then added three decorative buttons and but-tonholes along the stitched hemline.

———

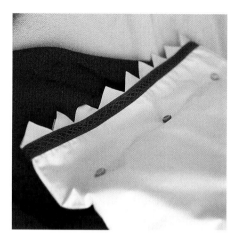

For a child's pillowcase, select a multicolored cotton ribbon with colorful childlike motifs and large buttons in primary colors.

MATERIALS

- **One standard-size pillowcase**
- **One standard-size pillow**
- **2yd (1.8m) of 1½in-(4cm)-wide washable yellow ribbon**
- **1½yd (1.4m) of ⅞in-(2.2cm)-wide washable red ribbon**
- **1½yd (1.4m) of ⅞in-(2.2cm)-wide washable lavender crochet braid**
- **Three ¾in (1.9cm) buttons**
- **2 x 3in (5.1 x 7.6cm) washable iron-on interfacing**

YOU'LL ALSO NEED:

Ruler or tape measure; pins; sewing machine with zigzag attachment or built-in buttonhole capabilities; matching thread; scissors; hand-sewing needle; iron; ironing board; and masking tape

---

DESIGNER'S TIP

For a more modern effect, use black and white ribbon on a natural-colored pillowcase, and substitute buttons that resemble ivory and ebony.

Instructions

1. Prepare pillowcase. Remove manufacturer's label from pillowcase and press pillowcase.

2. Sew ribbon points. Cut yellow ribbon into eighteen 4in (10.2cm) pieces. Press each piece in half across grain to form 2in (5.1cm) folded pieces (see illustration A, page 79). Pin pieces together to make one long continuous strip of right-angled points. Using thread to match pillowcase, sew folded pieces (illustration B).

3. Attach ribbon points. Pin or tape ribbon strip to right side of pillowcase so right angles of strip fall diagonally at edge of hem. Stitch strip to pillowcase ⅛in (3.2mm) in from hem edge (illustration C). Trim away raw edges of points ⅛in (3.2mm) before stitching line.

4. Attach red ribbon. Thread top of machine with red thread to match ribbon and bobbin thread to match pillowcase. Position red ribbon on top of pointed ribbon strip and pin in place so short ends overlap and hem at a side seam of the pillowcase. Topstitch top edge of ribbon along top edge of pillowcase hem. Repeat to stitch bottom edge of ribbon in place, trapping raw edges of pointed ribbon underneath (illustration D).

5. Add crochet braid. Thread machine top and bottom with thread to match crochet braid. Topstitch braid on top of red ribbon as in step 4 (illustration E).

6. Add buttons and buttonholes. Mark center front of pillowcase at hem stitching line (approximately 4in [10.2cm] in from edge.) with pin. Mark 7in (17.8cm) to each side with pins. Divide interfacing into three equal pieces. On underside of pillowcase, iron on interfacing at pins to reinforce buttonholes. Using thread to match pillowcase, make a machine made buttonhole at each pin. Mark position for buttons, then sew in place (illustration F).

Making the Folded Ribbon Pillowcase

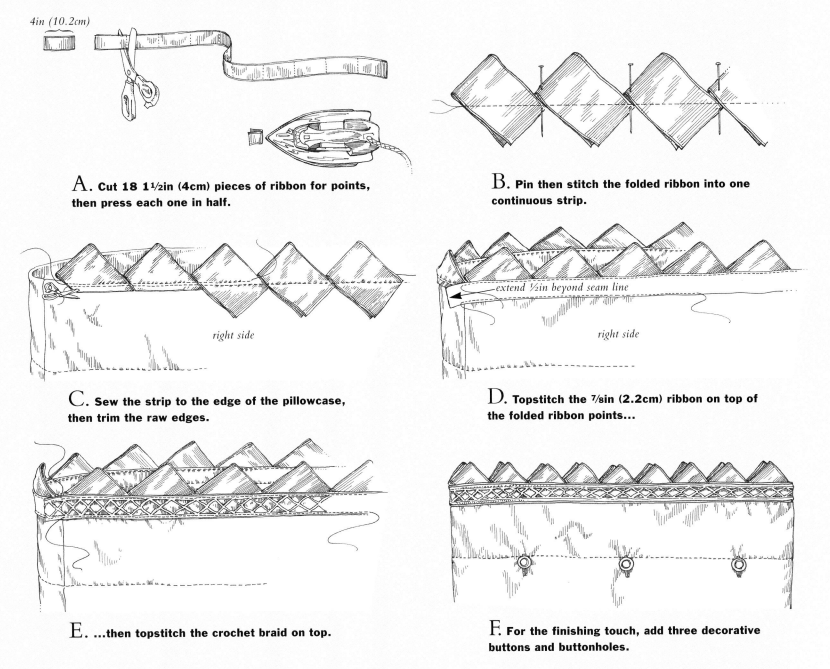

4in (10.2cm)

A. **Cut 18 1½in (4cm) pieces of ribbon for points, then press each one in half.**

B. **Pin then stitch the folded ribbon into one continuous strip.**

C. **Sew the strip to the edge of the pillowcase, then trim the raw edges.**

right side

D. **Topstitch the ⅞in (2.2cm) ribbon on top of the folded ribbon points...**

extend ½in beyond seam line

right side

E. **...then topstitch the crochet braid on top.**

F. **For the finishing touch, add three decorative buttons and buttonholes.**

Two-Color Pillowcases

Looking for a way to coordinate two mismatched pillowcases? We did just that by interchanging the hems of each pillowcase, then adding trim in between. We selected a white trim that resembles hemstitching, though it is actually made of narrow, crisscrossed ribbon. We backed the trim with pale lavender satin ribbon, which conceals the raw edges of the pillowcase on each side of the trim.

———

For a simpler version of this project, eliminate the ribbon backing, and just use the open, crisscross trim to attach the new hem to the pillowcase body.

MATERIALS

- **One 20 x 30in (50.8 x 76.2cm) key lime pillowcase**
- **One 20 x 30in (50.8 x 76.2cm) hydrangea pillowcase**
- **2½yd (2.3m) 1⅛in (3cm)-wide white crisscrossed trim**
- **2½yd (2.3m) 1¼in (3.3cm)-wide lavender satin ribbon**

YOU'LL ALSO NEED:

Sewing machine; thread to match pillowcases and satin ribbon; cutting shears; iron; and ironing board.

Instructions

1. Prepare pillowcases. Press pillowcases, cut out labels, and carefully cut off 4in (10.2cm) hems. If pillowcases have welting at hems, cut close to welting and above stitch holding hem (see illustration A, page 83).

2. Apply inset. Stitch raw edges of key lime hem piece together (illustration B). Position right side of trim along raw edge of hem (right side), leaving ¼in (6.4mm) extra trim at top. Stitch along raw edge using ⅛in (3.2mm) seam (illustration C). Overlap trim ¼in (6.4mm) when returning to start. Repeat with hydrangea hem.

Position unsewn edge of trim along raw edge of contrasting pillowcases (right side), then stitch in place as above using ⅛in (3.2mm) seams, and changing thread accordingly (illustration D). Press seams away from trim.

3. Apply ribbon backing. Turn key lime pillowcase right side out. Fold hydrangea hem back over pillowcase. Position lavender ribbon over trim, with ribbon extending ¹⁄₁₆in (1.6mm) beyond raw edges (illustration E). With hydrangea thread in needle and lavender thread in bobbin, stitch ¼in (6.4mm) below side seam using ⅛in (3.2mm) seams. Overlap ½in (1.3cm) when returning to start and fold ribbon inward for clean finish. Flip hem, right side showing, and topstitch ⅛in (3.2mm) from seam on hem fabric (illustration F). Repeat with hydrangea pillowcase, changing thread accordingly.

Making the Pillowcases

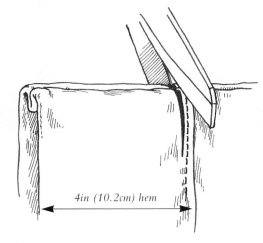

A. Cut the 4in (10.2cm) hem from the end of the pillowcases.

4in (10.2cm) hem

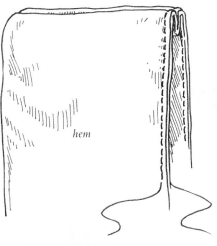

B. Sew the raw edges together to prevent slipping when the trim is applied.

hem

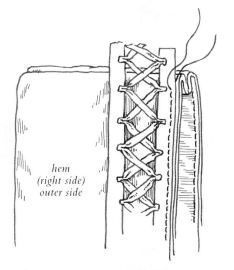

C. Sew the trim to the edge of the pillowcase hem, then fold the raw edge under.

hem (right side) outer side

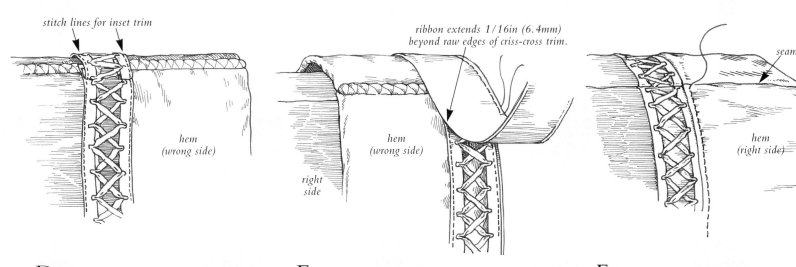

stitch lines for inset trim

hem (wrong side)

D. Stitch the trim to the corresponding edge of the pillowcase in the same way.

ribbon extends 1/16in (6.4mm) beyond raw edges of criss-cross trim.

hem (wrong side)

right side

E. To give the open, crisscross trim a backing, sew the ribbon over the trim.

seam

hem (right side)

F. Topstitch ⅛in (3.2cm) from the turned edges on each side of the trim.

83

bedroom accents

Hoop Canopy

Conjure up the soft breezes and tranquility of a tropical island in your bedroom with this sheer hoop canopy. This canopy uses a wooden embroidery hoop as its central support structure. The hoop holds the gathered fabric of the canopy in a circle, while nylon cords inserted in the hoop safely suspend the canopy above the bed. For best results, select a sheer, translucent fabric such as fine cotton, nylon, polyester, or netting.

———

Sticky-back Velcro comes with a sticky back hook portion, designed for hard surfaces such as the embroidery hoop, and a sew-on loop portion, which should be used on the canopy fabric.

MATERIALS

- 18in (46cm) wood embroidery hoop
- 2yd (1.8m) ¾in (19.1mm)-wide sticky-back Velcro®
- 10yd (9.1m) 45 to 56in (114.3 to 142.2cm)-wide sheer fabric
- 3yd (2.8m) cotton or nylon cord
- Large wooden bead at least 1in (2.5cm) in diameter and with ⅜in (9.5mm) threading hole
- ¾in (19.1mm) metal pot hook
- ½ to ¾in (12.7mm to 19.1mm)-wide double-sided tape
- 4 ⅔yd (4.3m) matching seam binding

YOU'LL ALSO NEED:

Scissors; cutting shears; tape measure; matching thread; sewing machine with size 11 needle; iron; and ironing board.

OPTIONAL ITEMS:

Gathering foot; fabric marking pencil; and 3 safety pins.

Instructions

1. Cut fabric. From sheer fabric, cut 3 pieces measuring 108in (2.7m) long. To make drapery, position two panels, right sides together. Stitch from top edge down 1½in (3.8cm). Repeat with third panel. Cut strip for ruffle measuring 7½ x 78in (19cm x

2m). Using hoop as template, draw and cut out circle of fabric measuring 20in (52cm) in diameter (diameter of hoop plus 1in [2.5cm] all around).

2. Assemble top circle. Stick double-sided tape around outside of hoop's inner ring. Stretch fabric circle over hoop's inner ring, pulling it tight. Trim any excess fabric below hoop rim. To mark placement of hanging cords, divide outside of inner ring into quarters and mark with pencil. Cut cord into four 20in (51cm) pieces; set aside remainder for central hanger. Knot one end of each piece. Place knotted end of cord just below bottom edge of inner ring at marks (see illustration A, facing page). (When the rings of the hoop are placed together, the knots will prevent the cords from pulling out.) Pin cords in place. Stick a second layer of double-sided tape all around outside of inner ring.

3. Prepare drapery. Measure fabric into quarters along top edge, and mark each quarter with safety pin placed 1in (2.5cm) below top raw edge. (Safety pins will correspond to quarter marks on hoop so gathers will be evenly distributed.) Turn bottom edge ½in (12.7mm) to wrong side twice to form hem, then topstitch. Press hem, then press out creases in main body of fabric. Cut seam tape to equal inner ring of hoop circumference plus 1in (2.5cm). Stitch ends together in ½in (12.7mm) seam to form circle. Divide tape circle into quarters and mark. With right side of drape facing out and wrong side of seam tape facing in, match drape marks to tape marks, then pleat or gather drape evenly between markings to remove fullness.

4. Assemble canopy. Adjust gathered fabric around inner hoop; match center back of drapery to screw at back of hoop, line up safety pins with quarter marks on hoop, and do not let raw edges of drapery show above edge of hoop rim. Cords should stick up from hoop as in illustration A. Stick fabric to double-sided tape, then place outer ring on top, securing gathered fabric and cords inside. Tighten screw (illustration B).

5. Make ruffle. With right sides together, stitch short ends of ruffle using ¼in (6.4mm) seam. Press seam allowance to one side. Turn piece with wrong sides together and stitch again, ½in

(12.7mm) from seam line and encasing first row of stitching and raw edges within new seam. Press, then topstitch double ½in (12.7mm) hem at bottom of ruffle. Lightly gather top of ruffle, reducing 76½in (1.9m) to 65in (1.6m). (This allows 5in [12.7cm] more than actual outer hoop size in order to fit fabric around screw.) Attach seam binding to gathered edge of ruffle as in Step 3.

6. Add frill to hoop. Stick hook portion of Velcro on outside of inner hoop, stopping at screw. Starting at ruffle seam, sew loop portion of Velcro onto right side of ruffle's top edge (illustration

C). Line up ruffle's seam with hoop screw. Fold upper edge of ruffle (including loop portion of Velcro) to inside of ruffle, then press two sides of Velcro together (illustration D).

7. Suspend canopy. Determine canopy height. Cut four cords on hoop to this length minus 3in (7.6cm). Thread four cords through bead, then make tight knots above bead. To make hanging loop, double 9in (23.3cm) length of cord into loop, knot ends, and thread through bead from bottom up (illustration E). Screw pot hook into ceiling and hang canopy (illustration F).

Making the Hoop Canopy

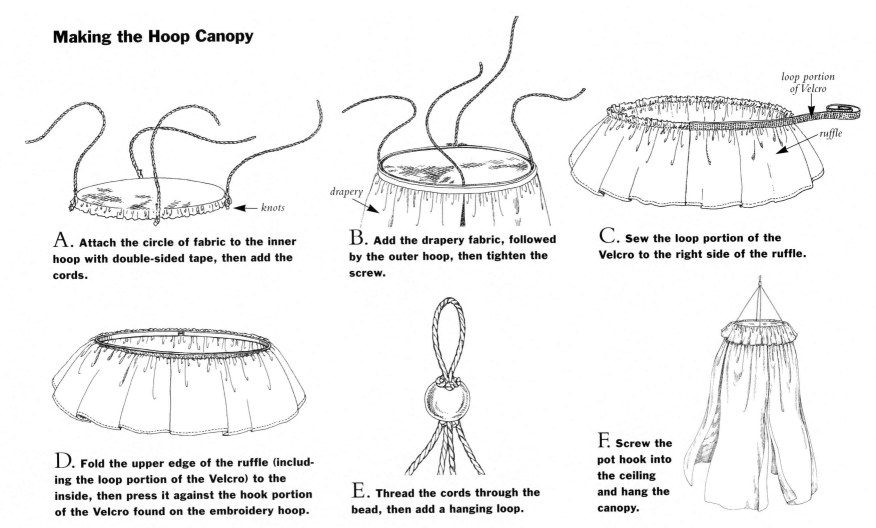

A. **Attach the circle of fabric to the inner hoop with double-sided tape, then add the cords.**

B. **Add the drapery fabric, followed by the outer hoop, then tighten the screw.**

C. **Sew the loop portion of the Velcro to the right side of the ruffle.**

D. **Fold the upper edge of the ruffle (including the loop portion of the Velcro) to the inside, then press it against the hook portion of the Velcro found on the embroidery hoop.**

E. **Thread the cords through the bead, then add a hanging loop.**

F. **Screw the pot hook into the ceiling and hang the canopy.**

Faux Four-Poster Bed

This faux four-poster effect, created with lightweight drapery fabric, will turn an ordinary bed into the main focus of a room. Although it may look complicated, the effect is actually quick and easy to achieve. Start by sewing a matching pair of scarves from a lightweight, gauzy material. Trim each end of the scarf so it comes to a point, then add a lightweight tassel. To assemble the four-poster drapery, insert pot hooks at four points above the bed, then hang a wooden curtain ring from each hook. The fabric scarves are threaded through the rings, crossing at the center point, to hang down at each corner of the bed.

—

For variation on this design, add a fifth hook in the center of the bed and thread both scarves through it.

MATERIALS

- **45 to 60in (1.1 to 1.5m)-wide lightweight fabric***
- **4 small tassels**
- **4 wooden curtain rings**
- **4 small pot hooks (or 4 sturdy cup hooks)**
 ***Note: See Step 2 to determine yardage.**

YOU'LL ALSO NEED:

Sewing machine; matching thread; yardstick or tape measure; pencil; cutting shears or rotary cutter and cutting mat; and hand-sewing needle.

OPTIONAL ITEMS:

5yd (4.6m) narrow trim (for covering hem stitches); double-sided tape (for securing draperies in curtain rings).

Instructions

1. Attach hooks to ceiling. Measure and mark points on ceiling exactly above bed corners. Screw pot hooks into marks.

2. Calculate fabric yardage. To determine required yardage, measure from one corner hook to hook at diagonally opposite corner. Add 10in (25.4cm) to this measurement and note as measurement A. Measure from lower inner edge of ring to desired length or drop of drape at headboard and note as measurement B. Repeat technique to measure drop at footboard ring and note as measurement C. Add A, B, and C measurements to obtain total required yardage (see illustration A, facing page).

3. Cut and sew scarves. Fold fabric in half lengthwise and cut to make two long, straight scarves. Lay pieces side by side on flat cutting surface. Mark and cut ends at 45-degree angle for points (illustration B). Staystitch ¼in (6.4mm) around all edges to prevent stretching. Topstitch, taking care not to stretch on bias at point. If desired, pin then topstitch edging on points to cover hem stitches. Sew small tassel at each point.

4. Assemble four-poster drapery. Pull one scarf through two rings. Hang one ring at headboard hook; hang second ring at footboard hook. Adjust fabric to drape as desired. Repeat process with second scarf and two remaining hooks. Arrange fabric in swags (Illustration C). If scarves slip in rings, use double-sided tape to secure.

Making the Faux Four-Poster Bed

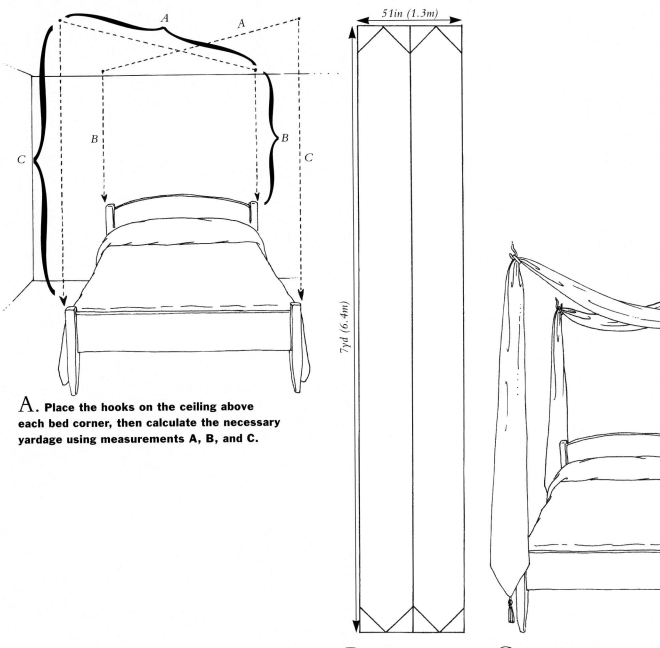

A. Place the hooks on the ceiling above each bed corner, then calculate the necessary yardage using measurements A, B, and C.

51in (1.3m)

7yd (6.4m)

B. Cut points on both ends of each scarf at a 45-degree angle.

C. Arrange the drapery in graceful swags.

Headboard and Footboard Slipcase

You can update your existing bedroom decor or give an unsightly bed a new look with this matching set of headboard and footboard slipcases. All you need to get started on this project are brown paper (for making a pattern), 5yd (4.57m) of fabric, such as the heavyweight, natural textured cotton we used, and the usual sewing tools. The following materials list and instructions are given for matching head and footboard slipcases for a double (full) bed.

———

Slipcases for head- and foot-boards are made the same way. The slipcase simply pulls over the headboard, reaching as far as the bedding on the inner side, and almost to the floor on the outer side. The two sides of the slipcase (we refer to them as the inner and outer pieces) are attached to one another using a gusset, which accommodates the headboard's depth.

MATERIALS

- **5yd (4.57m) of 54in (1.4m)-wide upholstery fabric***
- **One roll brown paper**

  *Note: If you are using fabric with a large repeat that has to match, you will need 6½yd (5.9m) of fabric; if your bed is wider than 52in (1.3m), you will need 7yd (6.4m) of fabric.

YOU'LL ALSO NEED:

Matching thread; sewing machine; cutting shears or rotary cutter and cutting mat; straight pins; pencil; yardstick; tape measure; iron; ironing board; and masking tape.

Instructions

1. Make head- and footboard patterns. Tape brown paper in place and trace outline of outer headboard. Mark position of horizontal support bar. To make identical halves, fold template in half vertically and retrace as necessary. On large, flat work surface, lay template on new piece of brown paper. To make outer side of headboard pattern, add 1½in (4cm) along bottom for 1in (2.5cm) hem, and ½in (12.7mm) around remainder of pattern for seams. To mark placement for ties, make notches where horizontal support bar joins headboard. Use outer pattern to cut

identical pattern for inner headboard, but end pattern at horizontal support bar (see illustration A, facing page). Line up both patterns, then notch center of each for matching to boxing.

2. Make boxing pattern. To establish boxing size, measure thickness (depth) of headboard frame. To determine boxing length, measure around edge of outer headboard pattern. Boxing will be cut in three pieces: headboard top piece and 2 side pieces. For headboard top piece, cut pattern measuring depth of headboard plus 1in (2.5cm),(which includes ½in [12.7mm] seam allowances) by full width of fabric. Line up edge of boxing on outer headboard pattern, matching center marks. Mark headboard pattern where edge of boxing will end. Measure from this mark to bottom of hem on outer headboard; this establishes length of side boxing pieces. Using illustration B as reference, determine placement and make side boxing pattern measuring 1in (2.5cm) extra in width at top (to include ½in [12.7mm] seam allowances), and flared at bottom, as necessary, to accommodate changes in width.

3. Make footboard and boxing patterns. Repeat Steps 1 and 2 for footboard.

4. Cut fabric. Position pattern pieces on fabric (illustration C). Mark and cut, including notches for matching. Cut 8 ties measuring 14 x 3½in (35.5cm x 9cm).

5. Make ties. Fold ties lengthwise, right sides together. Sew ¼in (6.4mm) seam down long edges. Center seams and press open. Sew ¼in (6.4mm) seam across one end. Turn right side out and press (illustration D).

6. Assemble slipcase. Stitch a side to each side of headboard, right sides together, to form one long strip. Press seams open. On inner headboard piece, press lower edge to wrong side ½in (12.7mm), then again ½in (12.7mm) to form ½in (12.7mm) double hem across bottom. Topstitch hem. Pin and stitch ties to sides of inner headboard piece (illustration E) right sides together and with cut (raw) edges even. On outer headboard piece, position raw edges of ties at notches, right sides together, center seam of tie facing up, then stitch in place (illustration F). Position cen-

Making the Slipcase

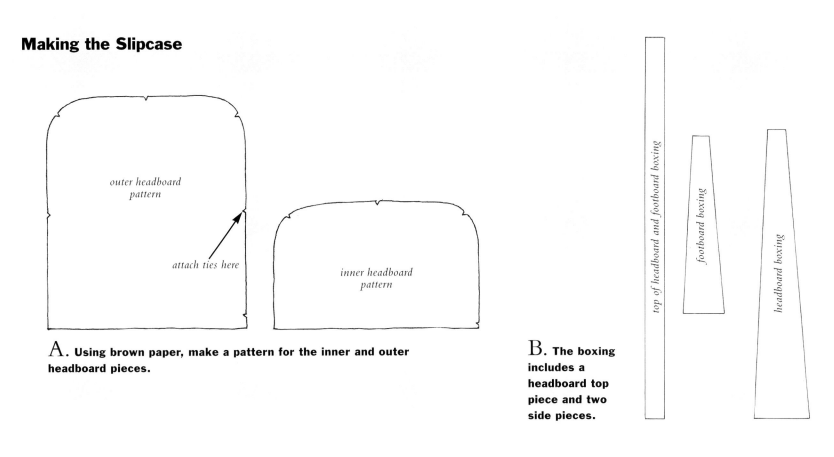

A. **Using brown paper, make a pattern for the inner and outer headboard pieces.**

B. **The boxing includes a headboard top piece and two side pieces.**

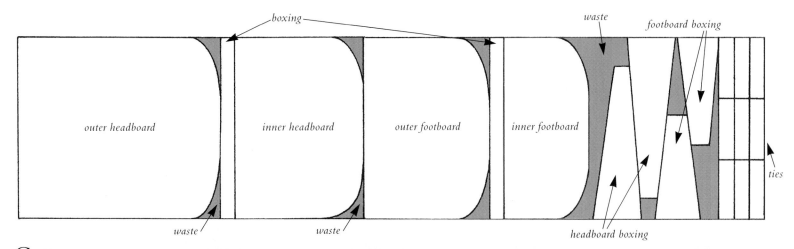

C. **For plain fabric and fabric with all-over pattern use the cutting layout shown here to cut the pieces for the slipcase.**
Note: If you are using fabric with a large repeat, you will need more fabric than is shown above.

If your headboard is upholstered and rounded, use muslin to make your template. Pin and mark with pencil darts or gathers to form a more tailored shape.

ter top of boxing strip on center top mark of outer headboard. Pin seams from top center point to hems on both sides, easing around curves. Stitch, using ½in (12.7mm) seams, trapping pinned ends of ties in boxing seams. Repeat to sew boxing and outer headboard to inner headboard piece (illustration G). Repeat process for footboard.

7. Finish slipcase. Try slipcase on headboard. Pin hem on outer headboard, which now includes boxing; hem should fall ½in (12.7mm) above floor. Press and topstitch. To make narrow hem along exposed side edges of boxing, press then stitch ¼in (6.4mm) hem. Repeat process on footboard.

DESIGNER'S TIP
For variation on this design, add welting, fringe, or another decorative edging.

Making the Ties

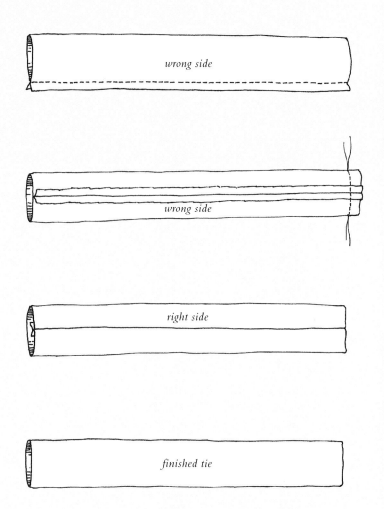

wrong side

wrong side

right side

finished tie

D. **Make eight ties—four for the headboard and four for the footboard—using the method shown.**

Finishing the Slipcase

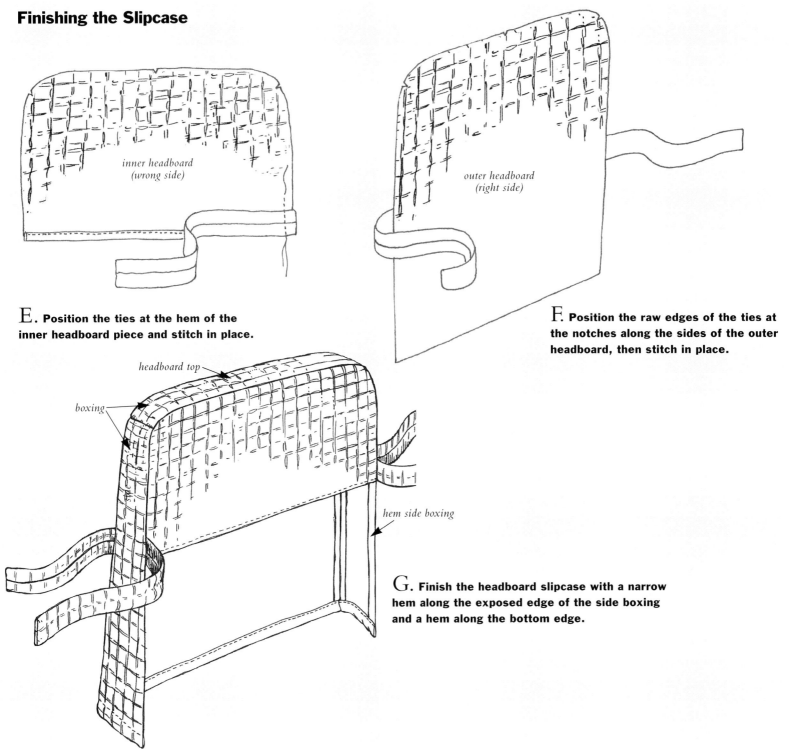

*inner headboard
(wrong side)*

*outer headboard
(right side)*

E. **Position the ties at the hem of the inner headboard piece and stitch in place.**

F. **Position the raw edges of the ties at the notches along the sides of the outer headboard, then stitch in place.**

headboard top

boxing

hem side boxing

G. **Finish the headboard slipcase with a narrow hem along the exposed edge of the side boxing and a hem along the bottom edge.**

Pinafore Chair Cover

You can create this country-style seat cover without using a pattern: Simply fit the fabric directly on your chair to create a box lid, then add sashes, which tie around the chair's posts to keep the cover in place. In general, the cover-up idea works best with small overall prints or solid colors. A larger or more pronounced pattern is not as suitable because the small area of the seat won't show off the pattern to its full advantage. You can use striped fabrics, although the overall effect is stronger and more lively when the stripes run diagonally across the ruffle. To do this, cut the fabric strips that make up the ruffle on the bias instead of on the straight grain.

—

The inspiration for this seat cover design comes from an old pinafore-style apron. For variation on this design, use contrasting fabric for the ruffle and ribbon for sashes.

MATERIALS

- **Chair (cross-rail back)**
- **2⅛ yards (1.9m) 45in (114.3cm)-wide cotton fabric**
- **Thread to match fabric**
- **Heavy-duty thread in contrasting color**

YOU'LL ALSO NEED:

sewing machine; iron; shears; rotary cutter; rotary cutting guide marked for 45-degree angle; dust-free chalk; clear acrylic ruler; pins; pencil and paper; pinking shears; and dressmaker's tape measure.

Instructions
Cutting the Fabric

1. Measure chair seat. Using tape measure, take the following seat measurements (see illustration A, facing page): (a) from front to back, beginning and ending at apron edge; (b) across widest part of seat at front, beginning and ending at apron edge; (c) around seat front and sides, beginning and ending at back posts; and (d) slightly beyond back posts. Jot down all measurements.

2. Cut basic slipcover pieces. Refer to Sample Cutting Layout (see next page) and use rotary cutter. Lay fabric flat, right side up. At one corner of fabric, cut seat rectangle measuring (a + 1in ([2.5cm]) x (b + 1in ([2.5cm]). For sashes, cut four 6in (15.2cm) x 54in (137.2cm) strips. For ruffle, cut two strips measuring 7in (17.8cm) x (1.25 x c). Then cut one strip measuring 7in (17.8cm) x (2.5 x d). Set aside remaining fabric for facings.

3. Miter-cut sash and ruffle strips. Stack sash strips so two face up and two face down. On top piece, make mark dividing 54in (137.2cm) edges into 30in (76.2cm) and 24in (61cm) segments; reverse mark on opposite edge. Cut diagonally between marks to yield eight miter-cut sash strips. Stack two longer ruffle strips face up. Using 45-degree mark on cutting guide, miter-cut strips at one end as in Sample Cutting Layout.

Fitting the Seat

1. Pin-fit seat front. Center seat rectangle right side up on chair seat; fold back corners diagonally from posts so fabric lies flat. Tuck and pin front corners (illustration B).

2. Rough-cut seat front to fit around posts. Using shears, cut diagonally into each folded-back corner to inner chair post (cut #1, illustration C). Fold fabric flaps up against post and make cuts #2 and 3, illustrations D and E. Allow fabric to relax and hang down against side and back of chair. Rub chalk along fabric to mark where seat cover and ruffle will meet. Trim off corners below front tucks. Remove pins and finger-press tucks to mark them.

3. Complete post cutaways. Lift fabric from chair and lay flat. Using chalk, draw line from back edge to side edge ¼in (6.4mm) inside cuts #1, 2, and 3; curve gently around corner (illustration F). To ensure symmetry, fold fabric in half and pin; make cut #4 on seam allowance through both layers. Trim rounded front corners, and clip into fabric edge a scant ¼in (6.4mm) to mark front tuck folds (illustration G).

4. Mark and cut two facings. Place reserved fabric right side up on work surface. Lay folded seat fabric on reserved fabric as template and draw chalk line along cutaway edge and back and

Sample Cutting Layout

Cut out the appropriate size fabric pieces using a rotary cutter. Stack the strips to make the miter cuts.

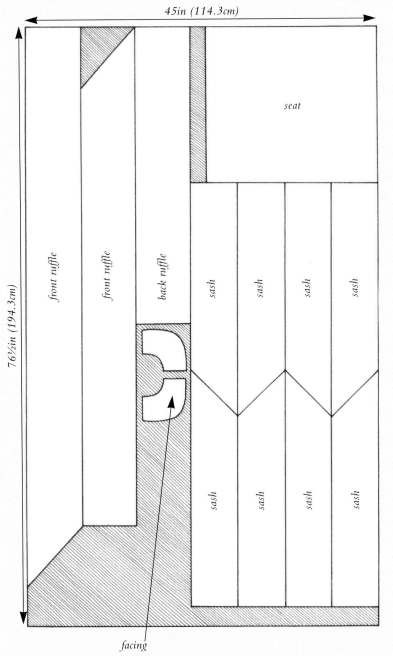

45in (114.3cm)

76½in (194.3cm)

front ruffle

front ruffle

back ruffle

seat

sash

sash

sash

sash

sash

sash

sash

sash

facing

Making the Chair Cover

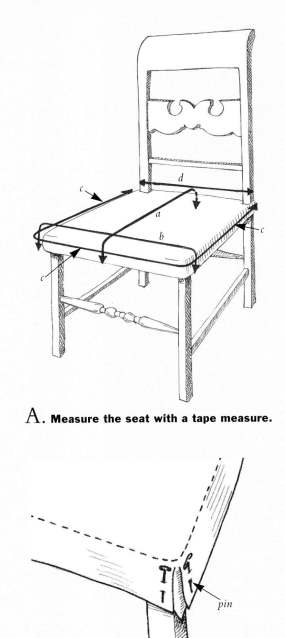

A. **Measure the seat with a tape measure.**

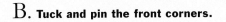

pin

B. **Tuck and pin the front corners.**

103

side edges for 2½in (6.4cm). Remove folded seat fabric. Measure and mark reserved fabric 2½in (6.4cm) from marked line for each corner piece to complete facing outline. Cut on marked outline to make two facing pieces in mirror image (illustration H). Clean finish raw edge using one of these three methods: narrow hem, pink and stay stitch edges, or zig-zag raw edges close to edge.

Sewing and Assembly

1. Sew four sashes. Pin eight sash strips right sides together in pairs. Machine-stitch ½in (12.7mm) from edge on long and diagonal edges; leave short end open. Clip corners, turn right side out, and press.

2. Sew front and back ruffles. Join two front ruffle strips by sewing diagonal edges together; press seam open. Fold each ruffle strip in half lengthwise right side in, and stitch short ends. Turn strip right side out and press with raw edges matching. Using heavy-duty thread, machine-baste ⅜in (9.5mm) and ⅝in (15.9mm) from raw edges. Draw up bobbin threads to gather.

3. Join sashes, ruffles, and facings to seat. Repin seat corner tucks to match clips and machine-baste ½in (12.7mm) from edge. Pleat open end of each sash accordion-style to measure 1½in (3.8cm) (illustration I, detail), then machine-baste to cutout edge of right side of seat fabric ½in (12.7mm) in from back and side edges (illustration I). Fold sashes onto center of seat, then pin front and back ruffles to seat edge, adjusting gathers to fit; allow ½in (12.7mm) between ruffle ends and cutout edge for facing (illustration J). Pin facings right side down on cutout edge. Machine-stitch through all layers ½in (12.7mm) from edge all around (illustration K).

4. Fit finished cover on chair. Clip corners and into curves, then turn slipcover right side out and press. Fit onto chair seat and tie sashes around posts in bows (illustration L).

Finishing the Chair Cover

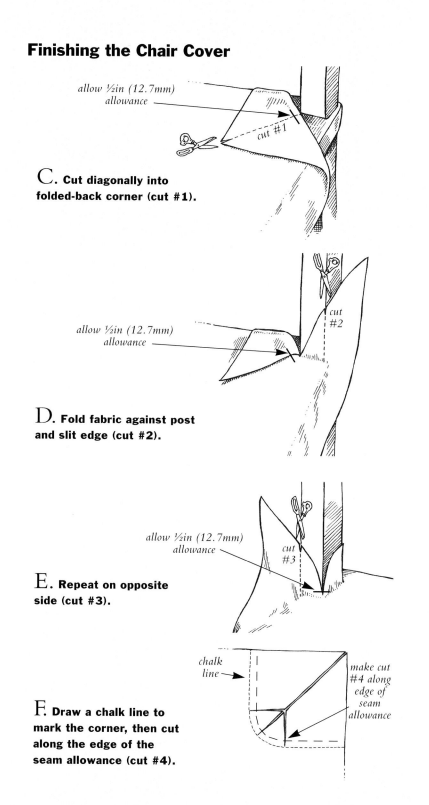

allow ½in (12.7mm) allowance

C. **Cut diagonally into folded-back corner (cut #1).**

allow ½in (12.7mm) allowance

cut #2

D. **Fold fabric against post and slit edge (cut #2).**

allow ½in (12.7mm) allowance

cut #3

E. **Repeat on opposite side (cut #3).**

chalk line

make cut #4 along edge of seam allowance

F. **Draw a chalk line to mark the corner, then cut along the edge of the seam allowance (cut #4).**

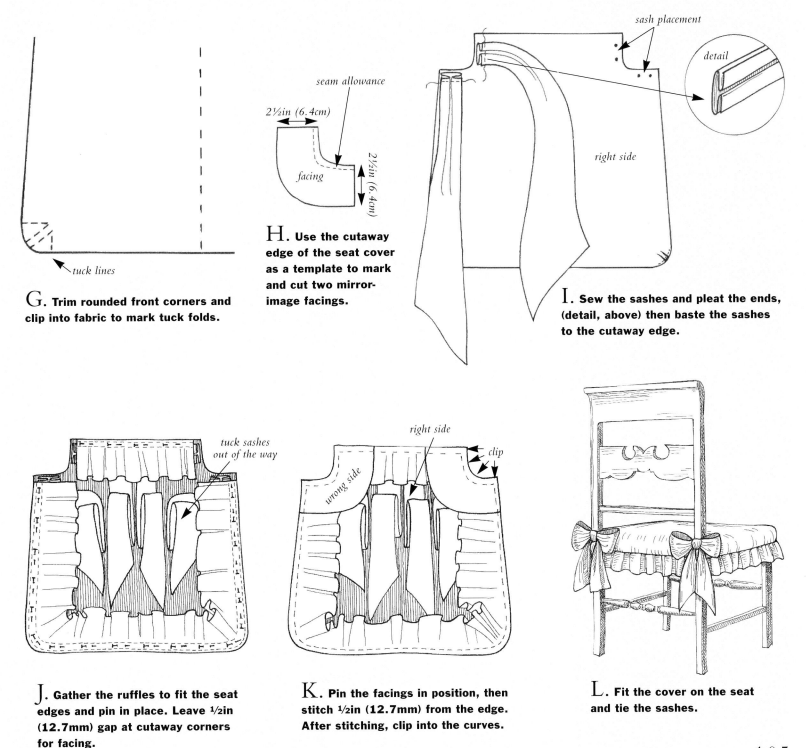

tuck lines

G. Trim rounded front corners and clip into fabric to mark tuck folds.

seam allowance

2½in (6.4cm)

2½in (6.4cm)

facing

H. Use the cutaway edge of the seat cover as a template to mark and cut two mirror-image facings.

sash placement

detail

right side

I. Sew the sashes and pleat the ends, (detail, above) then baste the sashes to the cutaway edge.

tuck sashes out of the way

J. Gather the ruffles to fit the seat edges and pin in place. Leave ½in (12.7mm) gap at cutaway corners for facing.

right side

wrong side

clip

K. Pin the facings in position, then stitch ½in (12.7mm) from the edge. After stitching, clip into the curves.

L. Fit the cover on the seat and tie the sashes.

Lace-Edged Bureau Scarf

Simple, square cocktail napkins make a perfect "fabric" for this handsome dresser scarf. We selected 12in (30.5cm), 100 percent cotton napkins with a simple band of hemstitching along all four sides, then joined the napkins with washable velvet ribbon. You can substitute napkins that have been hemstitched or embellished in other ways, napkins of different colors and fabrics, or even handkerchiefs. You can also substitute wider trim, but the assembly principle remains the same.

———

To custom-fit the scarf to your dresser, measure the width and length of the dresser surface, then shop for napkins or fabric that leave 1-2in (2.5-5.1cm) of dresser bare along the width.

MATERIALS

- **Three 12in (30.5cm) cocktail napkins**
- **3¾yd (3.4m) ¾in (19.1mm)-wide washable, double-edged eyelet lace**
- **3¾yd (3.4m) ¼in (6.4mm)-wide washable velvet ribbon**

YOU'LL ALSO NEED:

Sewing machine; matching thread; scissors; small safety pin; iron; and ironing board.

DESIGNER'S TIP

There are several easy ways to create variations on this design. Start by substituting colored napkins, squares of contrasting fabric, or lace handkerchiefs. Then select a new, matching trim to join the squares; eyelet for a country look, lace for a more romantic look.

Instructions

1. Prepare napkins. Remove all labels and press napkins. Place napkins in row, with grain running in same direction.

2. Sew eyelet between napkins. Trim threads that protrude from eyelet. Select line in design of eyelet to use as guide for top-stitching. Pin eyelet between first and second napkins, starting and finishing with same section of design; overlap eyelet equal distance on each edge of napkin, and let eyelet protrude ¾in (19.1mm) beyond top and bottom edges. Topstitch eyelet in place, taking care not to stitch over lace insertion holes (illustration A, facing page). Repeat between second and third napkins.

3. Thread velvet ribbon. Using small safety pin, thread velvet ribbon through each section of eyelet, then machine-stitch each end of ribbon (illustration B).

4. Sew eyelet around scarf edges. Using same line of eyelet design used for previous stitching guide, sew eyelet around perimeter of scarf. Start at one corner, leaving enough eyelet protruding beyond corner to form miter when you return to corner. Sew on inside edge of eyelet only. Fold eyelet to form miters at each corner. Disguise seam at final corner in fold of miter (illustration C).

5. Add ribbon to border. Using small safety pin, thread velvet ribbon through eyelet to finish scarf (illustration D). Secure ends with machine stitching, then press.

Making the Bureau Scarf

A. Arrange the napkins in a row, matching the grain direction. Sew the eyelet between the napkins.

B. Add the velvet ribbon and machine stitch to secure.

C. Sew the eyelet to form the border, mitering at the corners.

D. Insert the velvet ribbon around the border.

Velvet Floor Cloth

Getting out of bed will be easy when you step onto this multicolored velvet floor cloth. Assembled from seven different colored patches of upholstery-weight velvet, this luxurious floor cloth can stand up to a surprising amount of wear. To make the floor cloth, cut out five patches from each color of velvet, and lay them out in a grid. Sew the patches together to form columns, then sew the columns together. Next, sew on the border and corner squares. Last, add a linen backing to give the cloth firm footing and a neat finish. To prevent the floor cloth from slipping, use a non-skid rug backing under it.

———

The direction of the pile is important in this project. On the vertical grain, parallel to the selvage, velvet will stroke smoothly in one direction and roughly in the other. The resulting color and texture variance is less pronounced across the grain. Be sure that all the pieces in this project have their pile running in the same direction. One easy way to indicate pile direction is by marking each piece.

MATERIALS

- **Six ¼yd (.2m) lengths 50 to 60in (1.3 to 1.5m)-wide upholstery-weight, each piece in a different color**
- **1¾yd (1.6m) 50 to 60in (1.3 to 1.5m)-wide upholstery-weight velvet in a seventh color (for border)**
- **2yd (1.8m) 58 to 60in (1.5m)-wide linen backing**

YOU'LL ALSO NEED:

Sewing machine; thread to match border and backing colors; cutting shears or rotary cutter and mat; scissors; iron; ironing board; light and dark marking pencils; and yardstick.

OPTIONAL ITEMS:

Velvet-pressing board or scrap piece of velvet; and non-skid rug backing.

Instructions

1. Cut velvet patches. On flat surface, position each color of velvet in turn, right side down, making sure pile of each piece faces same direction. With contrasting colored pencil, mark five 9in (23cm) squares on each piece, indicate direction of nap with an arrow, then cut.

2. Lay out squares. Place cut squares in five columns of seven squares each, following grid design (see illustration A, facing page). Be sure arrows are all pointing in same direction. Stack columns to prepare for sewing.

3. Sew columns. Sew squares together to form first column using ½in (12.7mm) seams. Lightly press all seams open on velvet-pressing board or scrap of velvet. Repeat for remaining four columns. Sew columns together one by one, then press seams open (illustration B).

4. Cut border pieces. Select two colors for border: one color for side strips and second color for corner squares. For side pieces, cut two strips 5 x 57in (12.7cm x 1.5m) along vertical grain. For top and bottom borders, cut two pieces 5 x 41in (12.7cm x 1m) along horizontal grain. To indicate pile direction, mark wrong side with arrow. For corners, cut four 5in (12.8cm) squares and mark pile direction.

5. Sew border. Sew top horizontal border to top row of patches, right sides facing and matching pile direction (illustration C). Repeat on bottom horizontal border. Sew corner squares to ends of vertical borders, matching pile (illustration D). Press seams open on board or scrap of velvet. Pin, then stitch two border pieces to sides of patchwork (illustration E). Press seams open.

6. Sew backing on patchwork. Place lining on large, flat surface, right side up. Position patchwork on top, right side down. Pin all around, then cut away excess lining. Stitch around all four edges using ½in (12.7mm) seams, leaving 12in (30.4cm) opening at center of one side for turning. Trim seams and clip corners. Turn right side out and slipstitch opening closed (illustration F). Press edge, making sure lining does not show on right side of floor cloth.

7. Secure lining. Position floorcloth face up. Place pins in seam groove or line between border and patchwork center area, and in seam grooves at corners. Use thread to match border in top spool, and thread to match lining in bobbin. To finish floor cloth, "stitch-in-the-ditch," machine sewing through seam line, joining patchwork border to backing (illustration G).

Making the Velvet Floorcloth

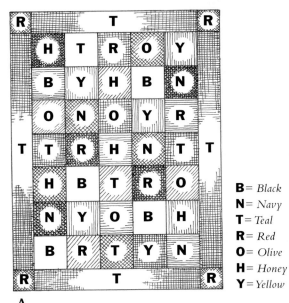

B = Black
N = Navy
T = Teal
R = Red
O = Olive
H = Honey
Y = Yellow

A. Arrange the squares of velvet in a patchwork arrangement.

B. Sew five columns of seven squares each, then sew the columns together.

C. Sew the borders to the top and bottom of the floor cloth.

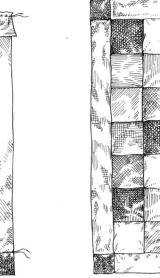

D. Attach the corner squares to the ends of the vertical borders...

E. ...then stitch the vertical borders along the sides of the floor cloth.

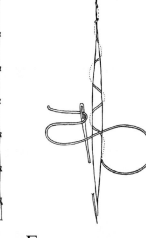

F. Attach the linen backing, turn the floor cloth right side out, and slip-stitch the opening closed.

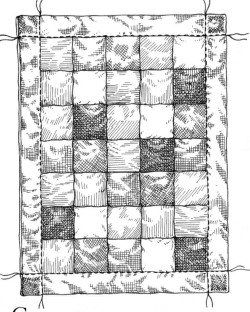

G. To stabilize the floor cloth, "stitch-in-the-ditch," machine sewing directly into border and corner seam lines.

113

Harvest Window Banner

This seasonal window banner, which features colorful autumn leaves scattered across a sheer, gold nylon panel, requires minimal sewing. Although the leaves look as though they've been appliquéd in place, we actually used fabric paint to fuse them onto the background fabric. The banner is designed to hang from an inexpensive tension rod much like a café curtain, except the banner is stretched taut to fill most of the window opening.

———

This window banner can be made to cover an entire window opening, or used to cover the lower half of a window with blinds in place.

MATERIALS

- **1 to 3yd (.9 to 2.7m) 45in (114.3cm)-wide metallic gold sheer nylon fabric (see step 1 to determine exact yardage)**
- **3⁄8yd (.3m) 45in (114.3cm)-wide sheer bronze lining fabric**
- **Sheer nylon remnants in any three fall colors (e.g., persimmon, plum, yellow-ochre, mustard, citron, rose madder, olive, or aubergine)**
- **Fabric paints to match remnant colors**
- **Thread to match banner fabrics**
- **Spring tension rod to fit window opening**
- **36 to 48in (91.4 to 121.9cm) long 3⁄8in (9.5mm) dowel (see step 5)**

YOU'LL ALSO NEED:

leaf patterns (see page 123); sewing machine; iron; cutting shears; steel measuring tape; small handsaw; light table (or use window during daylight hours); tweezers; freezer paper; newspaper; masking tape; sharp scissors; permanent marker; pencil and paper; and access to photocopier.

Instructions

1. Cut panel to size. Measure window opening width and height (as shown here, 42 x 68in [106.7 x 172.7cm]). Purchase sheer fabric yardage 8in (20.3cm) longer than window height (here, 68in [172.7cm] plus 8in [20.3cm] equals 76in [193cm], or about 2⅛yd [1.9m]). Subtract ½in (12.7mm) from original window width and 1in (2.5cm) from window height to determine finished panel size (here, 41½ x 67in [105.4 x 170.2cm]). Add 2in (5.1cm) to finished panel width and 6in (15.2cm) to finished panel length to determine cut panel size (here, 43½ x 73in [110.5 x 185.4cm]). Jot down all dimensions. Cut panel from sheer yardage to match panel size (here, 43½" x 73in [110.5 x 185.4cm]). Cut two strips from lining fabric that are equal to the finished panel width by 6in (15.2cm) long (here, 41½ x 6in [105.4 x 15.2cm]).

2. Sew sheer panel with channels. Press one long edge of each lining strip ½in (12.7mm) to wrong side. Lay panel wrong side up. Center lining strips along top and bottom edges, so panel extends 1in (2.5cm) at each side (see illustration A, facing page). Machine-stitch lining ½in (12.7mm) from raw edges of sheer panel (illustration A). Fold and press each side edge of panel ½in (12.7mm) to wrong side. Fold and press again, then topstitch to secure (illustration B). Fold top and bottom edges along stitching line, and press toward wrong side (illustration C). Fold top edge of panel to meet bottom edge of lining, then topstitch edge through all layers to secure (illustration D). Repeat on bottom of panel.

3. Prepare leaf appliqués. Make 12 photocopies of leaf appliqué pattern (see page 123), varying leaf size as desired. To vary final design, turn several copies face down against window (to see reverse image), and trace from wrong side with marker to make mirror image design. Tape patterns to flat work surface. Rough-cut a piece of sheer remnant for each leaf pattern, varying colors and sizes. Lay remnant over pattern, and tape down securely along edges; leaf will be visible through sheer overlay. Trace each leaf outline and spine with matching paint (illustra-

Sewing the Banner's Channels

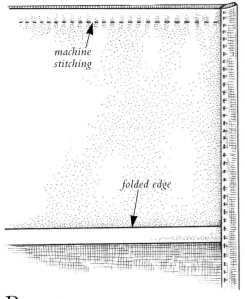

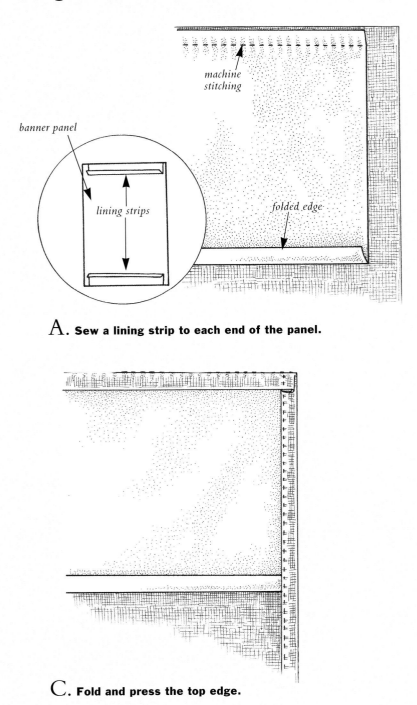

machine stitching

banner panel

lining strips

folded edge

A. **Sew a lining strip to each end of the panel.**

machine stitching

folded edge

B. **Hem each long side edge.**

C. **Fold and press the top edge.**

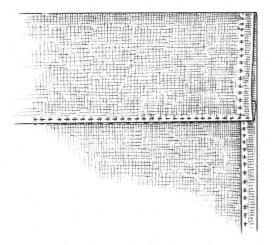

D. **Fold again and topstitch to form the channel.**

Prices for sheer fabrics range from $3 to $30 a yard, depending largely on the fiber content. The metallic fabric we purchased for $2.99 a yard is made from nylon, while pricier versions use silk. For this project, we found the nylon-based fabric easier to work with.

tion F). Let paint dry overnight or at least 12 hours. Remove tape. Cut out each leaf along paint outline (illustration G). Peel off paper pattern, using tweezers to pick off any paper that remains stuck.

4. Fuse appliqués to panel. Lay panel right side up on large work surface. Arrange leaves on lower half of panel, painted surface facing down; vary color placement and direction to create windblown look. Lay freezer paper (shiny side up) on top of newspaper, then slip freezer paper/newspaper padding underneath panel behind any leaf. Lay second sheet of freezer paper shiny side down on top of leaf. Set iron at lowest dry setting, then press gently to soften paint and fuse leaf to panel. Check progress after 1 minute; if fusing has not occurred, increase temperature one setting and try again. Repeat process to fuse all leaves to panel (illustration H). Let paint cool slightly before removing freezer paper.

5. Hang panel. Following manufacturer's directions, insert tension rod in top channel and mount in window opening. Saw dowel to measure panel width minus ½in (12.7mm). Insert dowel in bottom channel to hold panel steady.

Appliquéing the Leaves

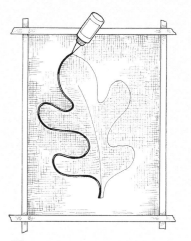

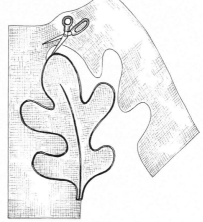

F. **Trace each leaf outline on sheer nylon with fabric paint.**

G. **When the paint is dry, cut out each leaf.**

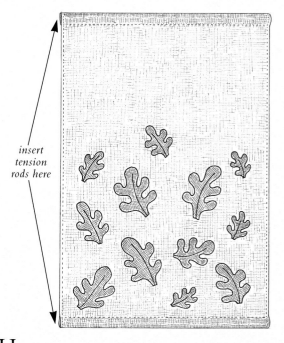

insert tension rods here

H. **Use an iron to fuse the leaves to the sheer panel.**

appendix

Glossary of Terms

Appliqué: Traditional method of attaching secondary pieces of fabric on top of a larger piece of fabric. Fabric is often fused in place, then topstitched around the edges using a zigzag or other decorative stitch.

Backing fabric: When using lightweight, non-upholstery fabric, such as dress fabric, for upholstering projects, it is important to back the fabric to give it more heft and body. Muslin makes a good backing fabric. Similar in concept to lining a dress or jacket.

Bias: Any diagonal that intersects the lengthwise or crosswise grain.

Button mold kit: Kit for making covered buttons. Includes a button shell, which is covered with fabric, and a button back, which holds the fabric in place over the shell.

Chiffon: Very lightweight, soft, sheer fabric, noted for draping ability. Originally made from silk but today generally made from artificial fibers.

Cutting shears: Scissors especially designed for cutting fabric or patterns, as angle of lower blade lets the fabric lie flat.

Damask: Firm, reversible fabric of jacquard weave, similar to brocade. Often used in home decorating.

Embroidery needle: Sharp, medium-length hand-sewing needle used primarily for embroidery.

Fabric glue stick: Fabric glue in a stick form, like lip balm.

Fabric marking pen or pencil: Designed for marking construction markings and alterations. Available in different forms, including chalk wedges, chalk in pencil form, and pens whose ink washes or fades away with time.

Finger press: To press a fold or section of fabric using one's fingers instead of an iron. Usually reserved for small areas or areas where a crisp fold is not necessary.

Fleece: A relatively new type of thick, warm fabric made from recycled plastic. Needs no hemming, but cannot really be ironed due to fiber content.

Furnishing-weight velvet: Also referred to as upholstery-weight velvet. A heavier, more durable grade of fabric; suitable for use on furnishings, where fabric is exposed to wear and tear.

Gauze: Open weave, sheer fabric made from many different fibers. Often used for curtains.

Grain: Most fabrics are made by weaving two or more threads at right angles to each other. Grain indicates the particular direction of the thread: lengthwise grain runs parallel to the selvage, while crosswise grain runs perpendicular to the selvage.

Hand baste: Hand basting (or tacking) is used to temporarily hold fabric together during construction.

Hand-sewing needle: A group of needles, most of them sharp needles, designed for general purpose sewing.

Hook-and-loop tape: A type of fastener featuring two tape strips, one with a looped nap and the other with a hooked nap. When pressed together, the surfaces grip and remain locked until pulled apart. Also called the brand name Velcro®.

Machine baste: Long, straight stitch used to hold fabric layers together during construction or permanent machine stitching.

Machine stitch: Using the sewing machine for a regular stitch length (10 to 15 stitches per inch [1.5 to 2.5mm]).

Matelassé: Luxurious, often jacquard weave fabric with raised design giving a puckered, quilted effect.

Mitered seams: Seams sewn on a mitered cut, usually a 45 degree angle.

Monofilament thread: Very thin transparent nylon thread used to make invisible stitches.

Muslin: Inexpensive cotton, made in a variety of weights, from gauzelike fabric to sheeting.

Muslin pattern: Often, before cutting an expensive fabric, it is advisable to make a pattern from muslin, an inexpensive cotton of plain weave. The pattern serves as a fitting shell to ensure proper dimensions and construction before cutting the actual fabric used for the project.

Pile (velvet): On the vertical grain, parallel to the selvage, velvet will stroke smoothly in one direction, and roughly in the other. If you are stroking across the grain, the color and texture variance is less noticeable. When working with velvet, all the pieces should have the pile running in the same direction.

Pinking shears: These special scissors cut a zigzag, fray-resistant edge. Best used for finishing seams and raw edges on fabric.

Raw edges: Cut or unsewn edges of fabric.

Right side, wrong side: Two sides of fabric; right side usually features pattern, wrong side is the side of the fabric that won't show once the project is completed.

Rotary cutter: A smaller version of the giant rotary cutters used by the garment industry, this cutting tool works like a pizza cutter and can be used by right- or left-handed sewers. Should be used with a cutting mat, which protects both the cutting surface and the blade.

Rough cut: Cutting fabric to a rough fit; leave about 2in (5cm) extra on larger projects; up to 3/4in (1.9cm) extra on smaller projects. Designed to reduce the amount of fabric without requiring an exact pattern or template.

Running stitch: A very short, even stitch used for fine seaming, tucking, mending, gathering, and other such delicate sewing. Resembles basting, except stitches are smaller and usually permanent.

Seam ripper: Handheld device featuring a sharp, curved edge for cutting seams open and picking out threads.

Selvage: A firmly woven strip formed along each lengthwise edge of the finished fabric.

Slipstitch: An almost invisible stitch formed by slipping the thread under a fold of fabric. It can be used to join two folded edges, or one folded edge to a flat surface.

Tapestry needle: Heavy, blunt-ended needles used mainly for tapestry work; can also replace a safety pin when threading a casing.

Topstitch: Machine stitches done from the right side of a project for decorative and/or functional reasons.

Trim or clip corners: Reduces bulk when points are turned right side out. Related variation: notching corners.

Trim seams: Cutting away some of the seam allowance, primarily to reduce bulk.

Zigzag: Locking stitch with a side-to-side width as well as a stitch length. A zigzag stitch features more give than a straight stitch, making it less subject to breakage.

APPENDIX

Patterns

Appliqué Blanket Turnover (see story, page 22)
NOTE: photocopy appliqué pieces at 200%

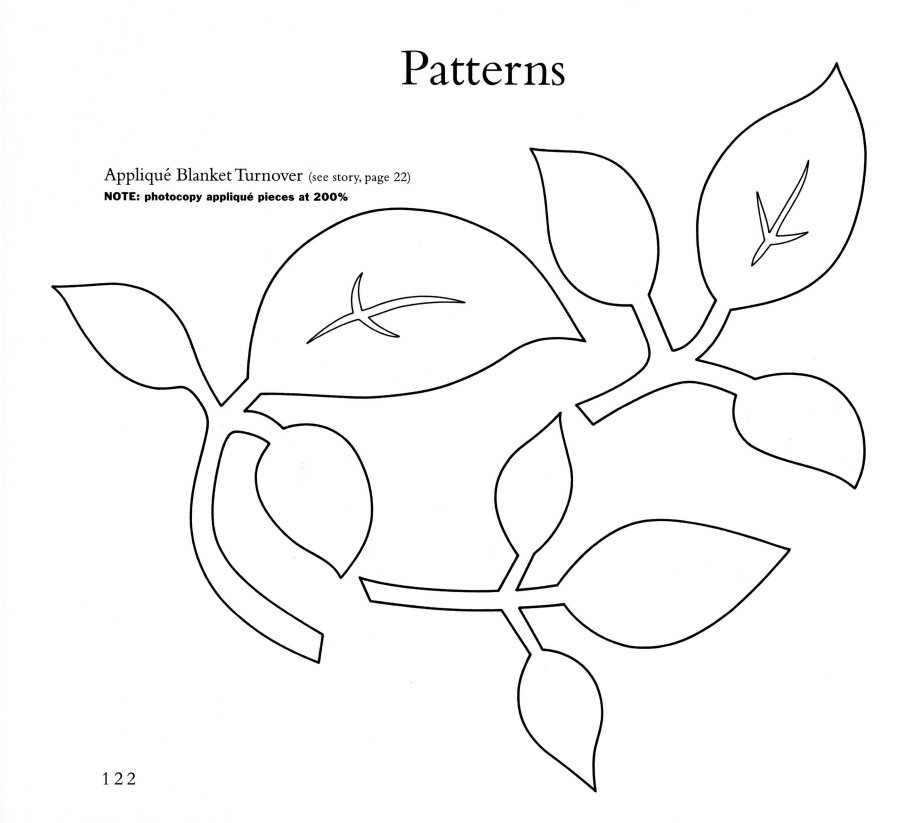

122

Harvest Window Banner (see story, page 114)
NOTE: photocopy leaf piece at 100%, or as desired

Sources

Contact each firm individually for an updated price list or catalog.

Atlanta Thread & Supply Company
695 Red Oak Road
Stockbridge, GA 30281
800-847-1001

Ballard Designs
1670 BeFoor Avenue NW
Atlanta, GA 30318-7528
800-367-2775 (orders) or
800-367-2810 (customer service)

Bed, Bath & Beyond
620 6th Avenue
New York, NY 10001
212-255-3550 or **800-462-3966**

Calico Corners
203 Gale Lane
Kennet Square, PA 19348-1764
800-213-6366

Chambers
Mail Order Dept.
P.O. Box 7841
San Francisco, CA 94120-7841
800-334-9790

Clotilde Inc.
Box 3000
Louisiana, MO 63353
800-772-2891

Coming Home
1 Lands' End Lane
Dodgeville, WI 53595-0001
800-345-3696

Crate & Barrel
P.O. Box 9059
Wheeling, IL 60090-9059
800-323-5461

Down Decor
Dept. SN, Box 4154
Cincinnati, OH 45204
800-792-3696

Gardeners Eden
P.O. Box 7307
San Francisco, CA 94120-7307
800-822-9600

Garnet Hill
Box 262, Main Street
Fraconia, NH 03580-0262
800-622-6216

Halcyon Yarn
12 School Street
Bath, ME 04530
800-341-0282

Herrschners Inc.
2800 Hoover Road
Stevens Point, WI 54492-0001
800-441-0838

Home-Sew
P.O. Box 4099
Bethlehem, PA 18018
610-867-3833

IKEA
IKEA Catalog Department
185 Discovery Drive
Colmar, PA 18915
800-434-4532

Keepsake Quilting
Route 25B
P.O. Box 1618
Centre Harbor, NH 03226-1618
800-865-9458

M&J Trimming
1008 6th Avenue
New York, NY 10018
212-391-6200

Nancy's Notions Ltd.
P.O. Box 683
Beaver Dam, WI 53916-0683
800-833-0690

Nasco Arts & Crafts
901 Janesville Avenue
P.O. Box 901
Fort Atkinson, WI 53538-0901
800-558-9595

Newark Dressmaker Supply
6473 Ruch Road
P.O. Box 20730
Lehigh Valley, PA 18002-0730
610-837-7500 or **800-736-6783**

Oppenheim's
P.O. Box 29
120 East Main Street
North Manchester, IN 46962-0052
800-461-6728

Oregon Tailor Supply Co., Inc.
2123 S.E. Division Street
P.O. Box 42284
Portland, OR 97242
800-678-2457

Pottery Barn
Mail Order Department
P.O. Box 7044
San Francisco, CA 94120-7044
800-922-5507

Sew/Fit Company
P.O. Box 397
Bedford Park, IL 60499
800-547-4739

Stretch & Sew Fabrics
8697 La Mesa Boulevard
La Mesa, CA 91941
619-589-8880

Sunrise Fabrics
264 West 40th Street
New York, NY 10018
212-768-7438

Thai Silks!
252 State Street
Los Altos, CA 94022
800-722-7455 or **800-221-7455 (CA)**

The Company Store
500 Park Plaza Drive
LaCrosse, WI 54601
800-285-3696

The Fabric Center
485 Electric Avenue
P.O. Box 8212
Fitchburg, MA 01420-8212
508-343-4402

Tinsel Trading Company
47 West 38th Street
New York, NY 10018
212-730-1030

Williams-Sonoma
Mail Order Department
P.O. Box 7456
San Francisco, CA 94120-7456
800-541-2233

Canadian Sources

The Cotton Patch
1717 Bedford Hwy
Bedford, NS B4W 1X3
902-861-2782

Bouclair
3149 Sources Bd.
Dollard-des-Ormeaux, QC
514-683-4711

La Maison de Calico
324 Lakeshore Blvd
Pointe Claire, QC H9S 4L7
514-695-0728

Omer DeSerres
334 Ste.-Catherine East
Montreal, QC H2X 1l7
800-363-0318 or **514-842-6637**

Rockland Textiles
2487 Kaladar Avenue
Ottawa, ON K1V 8B9
613-526-0333

Bouclair
1233 Donald Street
Ottawa, ON K1J 8W3
613-744-3982

Designer Fabric Outlet
1360 Queen St. W
Toronto, ON M6K 1L7
416-531-2810

The Fabric Cottage
16 Crowfoot Terrace NW
Calgary, AB T3G 4J8
403-241-3070

The Quilting Bee
1026 St. Mary's Rd
Winnipeg, MB R2M 3S6
204-254-7870

Homespun Craft Emporium
250A 2nd Avenue S
Saskatoon, SK S7K 1K9
306-652-3585

The Cloth Shop
4415 West 10th Avenue
Vancouver, BC V6R 2H8
604-224-1325

Acknowledgements and Credits

A collection of this scope requires the talents of many people. Generous thanks to those at *Handcraft Illustrated* who assisted in its preparation: Senior Editor Michio Ryan for his creative and technological acumen; Consulting Art Director Amy Klee, Art Director Elaine Hackney, Photographer Carl Tremblay, and Stylist Ritch Holben for manifesting the spirit and aesthetic attributes of each project; Editorial Assistant Melissa Nachatelo for the highest quality editorial support; Executive Editor Barbara Bourassa for intelligent and efficient project management and manuscript magic; and finally, Christopher Kimball, publisher of *Handcraft Illustrated*, whose original vision informed the work on all levels.

Several people outside *Handcraft Illustrated* also contributed to this work. Thanks to Chippy Irvine, not only for sewing many of the beautiful projects shown in this book, but also for writing directions and sketching illustrations. Special thanks, as well, to Judy Love for drawing such beautiful illustrations, and for helping us straighten out right side from wrong. And last, but not least, thanks to Angela Miller and Coleen O'Shea, of The Miller Agency, who believed in the project and gathered this creative team in an extraordinarily fulfilling process.

All the color photographs in this book were taken by Carl Tremblay. All the illustrations in this book were drawn by Judy Love, with the following exceptions: Tufted Napkin Quilt, Appliqué Scrollwork Blanket, Silk Ribbon Roses, and Harvest Window Banner, all by Mary Newell DePalma. Patterns by Roberta Frauwirth. Ritch Holben styled all the photographs in this book except for Silk Ribbon Roses, which was styled by Gabrielle Derrick de Papp/TEAM.

About Handcraft Illustrated

Handcraft Illustrated is a sophisticated, yet accessible how-to magazine featuring craft and home decorating projects. Each 52-page quarterly issue includes approximately 35 different projects. The projects are accompanied by a full-color photograph, a complete materials list, precise step-by-step directions, and concise hand-drawn illustrations. All projects featured in the magazine are fully tested to ensure that the readers can make the designer-quality craft projects at home.

Special departments include Quick Tips, an ongoing series of professional craft secrets, shortcuts, and techniques; Notes from Readers, a selection of detailed answers to readers' problems; Quick Home Accents, a unique pairing of materials and accessories designed to spur creative craft or decorating solutions; The Perfect Gift, an offering of creative solutions for designing, making, and packaging your own unique gifts; Quick Projects, a series of "theme-and-variation" projects featuring 4 to 6 versions of one easy-to-make craft; and Sources and Resources, a retail and mail-order directory for locating materials and supplies used in the issue.

For a free trial issue of *Handcraft Illustrated*, call 800-933-4447.

Index